The
Year
of the
Poet VIII

March 2021

The Poetry Posse

inner child press, ltd.

The Poetry Posse 2021

Gail Weston Shazor

Shareef Abdur Rasheed

Teresa E. Gallion

hülya n. yılmaz

Kimberly Burnham

Tzemin Ition Tsai

Elizabeth Esguerra Castillo

Jackie Davis Allen

Joe Paire

Caroline 'Ceri' Nazareno

Ashok K. Bhargava

Alicja Maria Kuberska

Swapna Behera

Albert 'Infinite' Carrasco

Eliza Segiet

William S. Peters, Sr.

~ * ~

In order to maintain each poet's authentic voice, this volume has not undergone the scrutiny of editing. Please take time to indulge each contributor for their own creativity and aspirations to convey their uniqueness.

hülya n. yılmaz, Ph.D.
Director of Editing ~
Inner Child Press International

General Information

The Year of the Poet VIII
March 2021 Edition

The Poetry Posse

1st Edition : 2021

Publisher Information
1st Edition : Inner Child Press
intouch@innerchildpress.com
www.innerchildpress.com

WHAT WOULD LIFE BE WITHOUT A LITTLE POETRY?

Dedication

This Book is dedicated to

Humanity, Peace & Poetry

the Power of the Pen

can effectuate change!

&

The Poetry Posse

past, present & future

our Patrons and Readers

the Spirit of our Everlasting Muse

In the darkness of my life
I heard the music
I danced . . .
and the Light appeared
and I dance

Janet P. Caldwell

Table of Contents

The Poetry Posse

Table of Contents . . . *continued*

March's Featured Poets   107

Inner Child News   145

Other Anthological Works   173

Foreword

Art just like literature more than ever acts as an instrument in spreading public awareness especially about issues plaguing our society. It is said that art should disturb the human psyche and should act as a catalyst for change.

Tatyana Fazklizadeh was coined as the "woman who waged an artistic war against her street harassers." She is an American activist, artist, and freelance illustrator. Fazklizadeh is the one behind the controversial "Stop Telling Women to Smile" street art project which strongly addresses gender-based street harassment which was first displayed in Brooklyn in the fall of 2012. The portraits depict different women who shared their sexual harassment experiences along with meaningful texts.

The artist powerfully voiced out one of the major sexual harassment against women issues through these captivating portraiture and was even made into a book. Sexual harassment should be actively addressed for this is continuously been experienced by women around the world. Fazklizadeh's masterpieces leaves a lasting impact and is a powerful way to be a voice of those women who choose to remain silent despite their sexual harassment experiences.

In this issue of the Year of the Poet, you will read powerful poetry coming from our talented and globally conscious poets depicting Fazklizadeh's artworks. Congratulations to my Poetry Posse Family again for a wonderful issue! Congratulations too to our awesome Featured Poets and we are thankful to all our loyal friends and supporters across the globe!

Elizabeth Esguerra Castillo
International Author and Poet

Preface

So, here we are, beginning our eighth year of monthly publication of *The Year of the Poet*. Amazing how much effort has been given by all the poets, to include the various members of *The Poetry Posse* and all the wonderful featured poets from all over our world. For myself, it has been and continues to be a great honor to be a part of this wonderful cooperative effort.

Last year, 2020 has been challenging for many of us throughout the year. We at *Inner Child Press International* were busy. We envisioned our role where the arts meet humanity to continue doing what we were good at . . . publishing. We managed to not only produce and publish this series, *The Year of the Poet* each month, but we were also very proactive in the arena of human and social consciousness. We were able to produce several other anthologies to include: World Healing, World Peace 2020; CORONA . . . social distancing; The Heart of a Poet; W.A.R. . . we are revolution; Poetry, the Best of 2020. Going forward, we are seeking to invest in the same or greater effort towards contributing to a 'conscious humanity'. We, poets and writers do have something to say about it all, and we intend to do so in any and every way we can. So stay tuned . . .

Bill

William S. Peters, Sr.

Publisher
Inner Child Press International

www.innerchildpress.com

PS

Do Not forget about the World Healing, World
Peace Poetry initiative for 2022. Mark your
calendars. Submissions will be opening . . .
September 1st 2021

Past volumes are vailable here

www.worldhealingworldpeacepoetry.com

**For Free Downloads of Previous Issues of
The Year of the Poet**

www.innerchildpress.com/the-year-of-the-poet

Tatyana Fazlalizadeh

March 2021

For Black History Month in the United States, we feature Tatyana Fazlalizadeh, an American artist, activist, and freelance illustrator is best known as the creator of the campaign and art exhibition *Stop Telling Women to Smile*. She was born October 12, 1985 in Oklahoma City, Oklahoma. She is also a featured artist for the NYC Commission on Human Rights DOT Art Program,

"I'll definitely pay attention to someone who is critiquing the artwork. But as far as someone not thinking street harassment is a big deal or that I'm being uptight? I don't think that's a valid critique."
~Tatyana Fazlalizadeh

NYC Commission on Human Rights DOT Art Program, Art Display Case (2019)

In partnership with NYC Commission on Human Rights and Tatyana Fazlalizadeh

"NYC Commission on Human Right's Public Artist in Residence (PAIR)" by Tatyana Fazlalizadeh at Sidewalk, Lenox Avenue between 124th Street and 125th Street, Manhattan

https://www.flickr.com/photos/nycstreets/48986699923

Poets . . .
sowing seeds in the
Conscious Garden of Life,
that those who have yet to come
may enjoy the Flowers.

Poets, Writers . . . know that we are the enchanting magicians that nourishes the seeds of dreams and thoughts . . . it is our words that entice the hearts and minds of others to believe there is something grand about the possibilities that life has to offer and our words tease it forth into action . . . for you are the Poet, the Writer to whom the Gift of Words has been entrusted . . .

~ wsp

poetry is . . . .

Poetry succeeds where instruction fails.

~ wsp

I FLY

because

... said the Dreamer to the world. I Can

www.iamjustbill.com

Gail Weston Shazor

Gail Weston Shazor

This is a creative promise ~ my pen will speak to and for the world. Enamored with letters and respectful of their power, I have been writing for most of my life. A mother, daughter, sister and grandmother I give what I have been given, greatfilledly.

Author of . . .

"An Overstanding of an Imperfect Love"
&
Notes from the Blue Roof

Lies My Grandfathers Told Me

available at Inner Child Press.

www.facebook.com/gailwestonshazor
www.innerchildpress.com/gail-weston-shazor
navypoet1@gmail.com

Cat Calls

Honey, did you hear that?
Something is cawing
On the other side of the street
Walking straight towards us
And then slinking away
I will ignore it
Just as little birds
Are afraid of cats
That caw should be
Struck down with fear
At a lioness
Such as I.

Why We Have Daughters

I want to take these things off you
The pride and beauty and pain
To strip you down to the time
When you were new
I would slowly brush your teeth
To rid them of the stains
From having bit the angry words back
I would have you cussing
Just to make the soft food taste better
A spoonful of not one more damn to give
Would surely smooth out the memories
Of being taken advantage of
And womanized and blackened
In the 60/70 incorporate
Push
I bathed my grandmother's worn out body
I did it with reverence and with notice
That her hands had bathed me many times
She smoothed the rough places with vaseline
And so I did the same, carefully
For I would not break the skin causing more lines
To add to the ones that living in a white world had
When she bit me, I cussed
And her eyes sparkled at
The fire she had just given me
That was her parting gift
And she knew that I would be a fighter
Just like her daughter
My child cusses
She really tries not to
But I make her mad sometimes

And often deliberately so
I just need to make sure
That before I too, go
To join my mothers beyond the veil
That she will have a lesson to share
With my ginger twin
And they will both be ok

Gold

I have said this to you
In both pretty words
And drawn out sighs
I have given you touches,
Just small intimacies
That shout my desire
In uncompromising want
And it is not that I cannot
Nor that I will not
But I have been patient
With feigned liberties
In a companionable time
As the lunar cycle
Wanes and waxes and crests
And the year eases into a full circle
I would have the experiences
That many must suppose
I already enjoy
Linked we as we are
Or
I would have the reasons
That stem the need
For prolonged discussions
Of this matter at hand
That I have summoned to form
In daydream and pillow wishes
I would that
Your breath gains mine
Hands across senses
With electricity arcing the wind
Head rolled back

Neck exposed
The very firmament moves
Against time
For here in this moment
Our moments have gained speed
On this path of passing time
And i would throw my freedom
Against ink and paper
To have you
As my claim

Alicja
Maria
Kuberska

.

Alicja Maria Kuberska – awarded Polish poetess, novelist, journalist, editor.

She is a member of the Polish Writers Associations in Warsaw, Poland and IWA Bogdani, Albania. She is also a member of directors' board of Soflay Literature Foundation, Our Poetry Archive (India) and Cultural Ambassador for Poland (Inner Child Press, USA)

Her poems have been published in numerous anthologies and magazines in : Poland, Czech Republic, Slovakia, Hungary,Ukraina, Belgium, Bulgaria, Albania, Spain, the UK, Italy, the USA, Canada, the UK, Argentina, Chile, Peru, Israel, Turkey, India, Uzbekistan, South Korea, Taiwan, China, Australia, South Africa, Zambia, Nigeria

She received two medals - the Nosside UNESCO Competition in Italy (2015) and European Academy of Science Arts and Letters in France (2017). Ahe also received a reward of international literary competition in Italy „ Tra le parole e 'elfinito" (2018). She was announced a poet of the 2017 year by Soflay Literature Foundation (2018).She also received : Bolesław Prus Prize Poland (2019), Culture Animator Poland (2019) and first prize Premio Internazionale di Poesia Poseidonia- Paestrum Italy (2019).

Be yourself

You have the right to feel fatigued
when the evening paints the shadows
 under your tired eyes .

Do not close your regret in silence
 - or it will explode like a volcano
and destroy your seemingly safe world.

Let nobody tell you to smile.
Sadness and bitterness are natural .
They sculpt your face as does your joy.

You are a woman - not a doll
with painted happiness on its face
and an emotionless gaze.

Addressee unknown
poem dedicated to Nabila Al – Amoodi

I have a few yellowed letters
and an album full of old photos.
I am storing our youth
- ambitious plans, laughter and tears.

Today I am surrounded by helplessness.
 Anxiety creeps in my mind
and longing in the words of the poem.

Where are you my friend?
Which side of heaven are you on?
Are there the flowers around your house in Sana,
or maybe there is only the dead earth?

 Unanswered questions
and searching without believing in a miracle
do not let me forget about you.

Yesterday you came back unexpectedly
- when I was looking at pictures of Yemeni children.
 In the eyes of a girl dying of hunger
I saw your portrait.

Buchenwald station

In a small suitcase
memories of happy days
and hope for a good fortune
can be packed carefully.

In one corner
there were photos
 - parents' concerned look
and love in the eyes of the girl
and next to them,
 a warm sweater and provisions.

A little cash and some gold
were hidden cleverly in a pocket.
The black hour has not come yet,
though it lurks every minute

Isaak breathed a sigh of relief
when the train stopped
in German Buchenwald
- it's not blasted Polish Auschwitz.

He left without hesitation
all his treasures for the promise
of a hot bath after a long journey.
He got a receipt for his suitcase.

Jackie
Davis
Allen

Jackie Davis Allen

Jackie Davis Allen, otherwise known as Jacqueline D. Allen or Jackie Allen, grew up in the Cumberland Mountains of Appalachia. As the next eldest daughter of a coal miner father and a stay at home mother, she was the first in her family to attend and graduate from college. Her siblings, in their own right, are accomplished, though she is the only one, to date, that has discovered the gift of writing.

Graduating from Radford University, with a Bachelors of Science degree in Early Education, she taught in both public and private schools. For over a decade she taught private art classes to children both in her home and at a local Art and Framing Shop where she also sold her original soft sculptured Victorian dolls and original christening gowns.

She resides in northern Virginia with her husband, taking much needed get-aways to their mountain home near the Blue Ridge Mountains, a place that evokes memories of days spent growing up in the Appalachian Mountains.

A lover of hats, she has worn many. Following marriage to her college sweetheart, and as wife, mother, grandmother, teacher, tutor, artist, writer, poet and crafter, she is a lover of art and antiques, surrounding herself, always, with books, seeking to learn more.

In 2015 she authored *Looking for Rainbows, Poetry, Prose and Art*, and in 2017, *Dark Side of the Moon*. Both books of mostly narrative poetry were published by Inner Child Press and were edited by hulya n. yilmaz.

in 2019, No Illusions.Through the Looking Glass, which was nominated to be considered for a Pulitzer Prize by the publisher and editor of InnerChild Press, ltd.

http://www.innerchildpress.com/jackie-davis-allen.php
jackiedavisallen.com

☐ You Telling Men the Same Thing?

Bite your lip. Endure the pain.
Suffer the humiliation. Say nothing.
Keep your thoughts locked
Up behind mask of a smile? Sometimes
A smile is the wiser course of action.

You think it did not faze me
When those construction workers
Whistled and jeered
As I sauntered past them? What say you?
Should I have smiled? Cried?

Again, I am told to just smile.
Well, I am female. I am all grown up.
I have learned what is expected of me.
Maybe that is why I think for myself? Thank you.
I will smile whenever I so choose.

A smile can help avoid conflict.
So, for safety's sake, I will, thank you,
I will smile whenever I want to.
Maybe that is why I am my own person? And why,
I try not to make an issue of being offended.

Alone in my Closet

The sacred echo
Reverberates in my mind
Silently convicting me
Of the duty and blessing

Of loving actively,
Of acknowledging the source
By which the gentle, persistent
Nudging of my heart

Instructs my conscious,
If you will, by faith alone
To heed the admonition
To love, to share, to do
That which is right.

A Quiet Place

Poetically speaking, I needed a break.
So, on a whim, I decided to meander
Down the hill, to the garden path,
Where there stood, over by the babbling brook
A grove of ancient cherry trees.

The sky was a blue bird blue. And I,
Glancing up, saw before me a plethora
Of sweet blossoms nodding their heads,
Clinging to the outstretched arms
Of the willing Japanese, cherry trees.

A flock of birds flew overhead.
A gentle breeze kissed my face; it caught
A wisp of my hair And as I brushed it away,
The sun began to hum and dance, in step,
With the shadows that were following me..

Tzemin
Ition
Tsai

Dr. Tzemin Ition Tsai (蔡澤民博士) was born in Republic of China, in 1957. He holds a Ph.D. in Chemical

Engineering and two Masters of Science in Applied Mathematics and Chemical Engineering. He is a professor at Asia University (Taiwan), editor of "Reading, Writing and Teaching" academic text. He also writes the long-term columns for Chinese Language Monthly in Taiwan.

He is a scholar with a wide range of expertise, while maintaining a common and positive interest in science, engineering and literature member. He is also an editor of "Reading, Writing and Teaching" academic text and a columnist for *'Chinese Language Monthly'* in Taiwan

He has won many national literary awards. His literary works have been anthologized and published in books, journals, and newspapers in more than 40 countries and have been translated into more than a dozen languages.

Street art

Has never been a wide street
Let it go
Weeping willow silk does not have a hundred feet
The middle school generation group rushes and has nothing
to do
Fighting for Street West Purple Peony
Just pushing
Pushing

Slanting street under the sunset
I didn't mean to be alarmed
The red-brick wall of North Street
Osmanthus shadow shift frequently urges time
The ripples of the spring water carry a chill like chaff
Ignore it
Tears invade the face leaving a slight redness
It's hard to update a woman's face with frown

Sophorae rain, the next is floating past fate
Combined face
That pair of black and white
The wall-painted roller hides like a fairy
White cloud ridicule
move so well and all I can do is let them go and hope
laugh
Stop harassment on the street, visible or invisible

When I thought of my Wheat Field

On that day my soul grew silent
Once I sat engaged and ricing
Only this and a oxeye daisy
In there stepped a silent 'paddy'
The grit brought such sorrow back into my memories
malting
So I threw my rye upon the floor

'Wheat!' chuckled I, 'Yes Wheat!'
The splendid sunflower on that day made my soul grew
happy
The grains I saw just in hat kingdom full of soybeans

'Wheat!' said I, 'thing of beet.'
My passion agricultural buckwheat
A lonely, splendid ricing
Awoke me and flung the dough
From a silent midnight
Much marveled the wheatworm sunflower

'Wheat!' said I, 'thing of cotton.'
Deep into that darkness gritting
My passion is the silent alfalfa
Wheat-worms, smelly baling
Much marveled the lonely sweet corn

Wheat - tormentor of my dreams
On that day my soul grew splendid

Lighthouse

Once upon a midnight leading me discovered the
lighthouses
The intertidal influential inducing me discovered the
islands
And its eyes have all the windmilling
Remembering many district, lonely shipwrights
The top tower triggering
Only this and a beach
Instead I uncovered the catboat
The lighthouse steped on the beach
Suddenly, I heard some off-shore
Take thy seascape from out my heart
I felt compelled to sniff the rookeries
The hidden strait voyage, the lights never leaking
es that are peeking
Long I stood there quietly
Pretending to be an ocean sunfish, and you are a houseboat
The coastal causeway conducting, I crave the sunlit, senior
seawall
The shorefront, sick sailboard
I was a shipwreck and you an idyll
I was a lamp and you a dinghy
And its eyes have all the suntanning
The barelegged brushwork bodysurfing

Shareef
Abdur
Rasheed

Shareef Abdur-Rasheed, AKA Zakir Flo was born and raised in Brooklyn, New York. His education includes Brooklyn College, Suffolk County Community College and Makkah, Saudi Arabia. He is a Veteran of the Viet Nam era, where in 1969 he reverted to his now reverently embraced Islamic Faith. He is very active in the Islamic community and beyond with his teachings, activism and his humanity.

Shareef's spiritual expression comes through the persona of "Zakir Flo" . Zakir is Arabic for "To remind". Never silent, Shareef Abdur-Rasheed is always dropping science, love, consciousness and signs of the time in rhyme.

Shareef is the Patriarch of the Abdur-Rasheed Family with 9 Children (6 Sons and 3 Daughters) and 41 Grandchildren (24 Boys and 17 Girls).

For more information about Shareef, visit his personal FaceBook Page at :

https://www.facebook.com/shareef.abdurrasheed1
https://zakirflo.wordpress.com

Tatyana

tell 'em tatyana
baaaad sister
shine the light
art be the flood light
address the plight
bring on the fight
we are somebody
not going nowhere
hey here to stay
Tatyana baaaaad sister
don't f with us mister
respect all my sisters
shed the light on canvas
brick walls on structures
address the disrespect
f*^k the hush up
sat it loud with the brush up
for sisters, brothers, humans
ostracized, demonized,
marginalized, sexualized,
even criminalized
Tatyana baaad sister
will check you mister

dem no respect?
your brush put 'em in check
don't tell us to smile
with your demeanor vile
AmeriKKKa is...black, brown
indigenous, latina, latino,
european, asian, straight

dem that ain't
ain't going nowhere
like Tatyana, baaad sister
f the hush she talks with a
brush

Contemplating..,

lost souls in a lost role
misguided can't hide it
walking earth in a fog
jerks,
frogs on a log
took easy way out
reflects what comes out
dem mouth
nothing to talk about
bull$#!+ repeated
sense deleted
self-defeated in lock step
worship devils embrace evil
roam earth for upheaval
misguided folk confined in
spiritual yoke self-imposed
due to arrogance growth
my folk better than your folk
no truth to the root
liars capture lost hearts
detached from facts
easy prey captured by con
don't have a clue what's going on
house built on sand
sinking fast
hate, fear, ignorance, unjust, lust
moral compass bust
in creation not creator
dem put trust
lost souls to highest bidder sold
ground to dust
control of few over rest of us
outcome: surrender soul to wrong one

darkness comes, blocked the sun
Ponder

Just amazing..,

how life with all twist, turns,
ups, downs propose challenge
after challenge
nothing is guaranteed
always need to strive to succeed
always need to plant righteous
seeds
separate wheat from weeds
what do i mean?
implying effort to be clean
of heart, mind, soul
implying the whole that
constitutes piety
require sincere intentions
can not fake real
complacency does not replace
real zeal
though fleeting this life
there is time to get it right
requires fire
burning deep within
i must fight to attain self
control
starve the flesh, feed the soul
when shaitan whispers into
the heart
you say no
i don't want to go where
you go
this can never be heaven, why?
to attain heaven, we must die
remember the old saying

" everybody wants to go to heaven
but nobody wants to die "?
remember all acquired here
possessions stacked,
bank accounts packed
mansions of generous proportion
creates misleading distortion
that it constitutes substance
notion evaporates when angel of death
takes your soul and all that you lived for
you then will know has no worth
no meaning anymore
never did from jump street
folk say "you can't take it with you "
but the way folk live for material pursuit
you would think they don't believe that's
true, just dropping lip service on you
you can only take your deeds with you
down underground alone
in that dark, cold hole called the grave
then known as home
righteous deeds and creator's mercy
is what you need to succeed to
go to heaven
now that's what you call substance
thinkaboutit

Kimberly Burnham

A brain health expert with a PhD in Integrative Medicine, Kimberly Burnham has lived in tropical Colombia; in Belgium during the Vietnam War; in Japan teaching businessmen English; in diverse international Toronto, Canada; and several places in the US. Now, she's in Spokane, WA with her wife, Elizabeth, two sets of twins (age 11 & 14) and three dogs. Her recent book, *Awakenings: Peace Dictionary, Language and the Mind, a Daily Brain Health Program* includes the word for peace in hundreds of languages. Her poetry weaves through 80+ volumes of *The Year of the Poet, Inspired by Gandhi, Women Building the World*, and *A Woman's Place in the Dictionary*. She is currently working on several ekphrastic writing projects. One is a novel, *Art Thief Cracks Healing Code for Parkinson's Disease* and the other is non-fiction, *Using Ekphrastic Fiction Writing and Poetry to Create Interest and Promote Artists, Writers, and Poets*.

http://www.NerveWhisperer.Solutions

https://healthy-brain.medium.com/bears-at-the-window-of-climate-change-d1fb403eeaf3

Perched on a Brick Wall

High above the heads of thoughts
passing by
a better view
my world
perched on a brick wall
a colorful spot
where every child has time
sight
and knowledge
to read
grow and write
lose ourselves in a book
climb out
make this a better world
for every child

Self-Reflection Haiku

myself reflected

in myriad nuanced ways

I define myself

Human Rights

Seeing images of people like me
should be a human right
my right to have role models
the way I look
how I think
about the world
reflected back

Your human right
also together
as we ponder
be the role model
we wish to see
uniquely inspire
each of us beautiful

Elizabeth E. Castillo

Elizabeth Esguerra Castillo is a multi-awarded and an Internationally-Published Contemporary Author/Poet and a Professional Writer / Creative Writer / Feature Writer / Journalist / Travel Writer from the Philippines. She has 2 published books, "Seasons of Emotions" (UK) and "Inner Reflections of the Muse", (USA). Elizabeth is also a co-author to more than 60 international anthologies in the USA, Canada, UK, Romania, India. She is a Contributing Editor of Inner Child Magazine, USA and an Advisory Board Member of Reflection Magazine, an international literary magazine. She is a member of the American Authors Association (AAA) and PEN International.

Web links:

Facebook Fan Page

https://free.facebook.com/ElizabethEsguerraCastillo

Google Plus

https://plus.google.com/u/0/+ElizabethCastillo

Respect Me

I don't compete with anybody else
I don't have to prove my worth to you
I am simply me
Free as a bird, free to live,
And I have rights you should respect.
As a woman, respect me
Like you do to your own mother
I don't have to earn it,
It is one of my rights
Don't think I'm all here for you.
Respect me, a woman
Not just an object of your desire,
I don't ask you to put me on a pedestal
For I am not a God,
I'm just human
But respect me as I do to you.

Nomads of Sahel

Blessed are you -
With your rugged terrain
Nestled in the Sahara Desert
In the long forgotten land of Mali.
In a brief sojourn, one can see-
The eclectic life of the Fulani
"Blue men of the desert" they are called
Clothed in mystic, indigo robes and turbans.
Children of Sahel -
Born in a semi-arid steppe country,
Running on dry soil, famished
Victims of civil war, drought, and large-scale migration.

Indigo Child

i am not of this world -
i came from an abysmal chaos-
but from this beautiful chaos, Desiderata was born-
a child of the Universe, precious and golden
a lovely old soul beyond time and space-
often misunderstood by mediocre minds-
but applauded by great free thinkers -
i long for a world enveloped in serenity-
inhabited by empaths with great sensitivity
a loner I may be but this is who I am-
but i've got this deep connection with things around me
an indigo girl at birth-
my temporary sanctuary is the Earth
lonewolves gather at my feet-
for i am their Goddess in human form.

Joe
Paire

Joseph L Paire' aka Joe DaVerbal Minddancer . . .
is a quiet man, born in a time where civil liberties
were a walk on thin ice. He's been a victim of his
own shyness often sidelined in his own quest for
love. He became the observer, charting life's path.
Taking note of the why, people do what they do.
His writings oft times strike a cord with the
dormant strings of the reader. His pen the rosined
bow drawn across the mind. He comes full-frontal
or in the subtlest way, always expressing in a way
that stimulate the senses.

www.facebook.com/joe.minddancer

WHO AM I?

I've often read the headlines before the author.
Can you read the taste of good beef?
Can you experience freezing cold on the equator?
So how can you say to her, don't be like that?

Is there something wrong with an image.
that it would change just knowing who the artist was
who they are, who they were, what side of humanity?
So how can I say to her, what medium to choose?

A little girl is a little girl, biblically speaking.
We tend to add action to colors we're not familiar with
That's how some paintings get destroyed.
over pigmented sin, by pigheaded men.

I saw my neighbors' kid, she's an odd one.
She dresses like a princess.
as she walks by the fence setters
cat callers with no age limits

A daily blemish for the un-held hand
The way we limit ourselves to the voice of man.
I helped raise a young woman who looks.
Exactly like the image before me, who is she?

No Closer To The Truth

How many sayings are there about telling the truth?
How many times, with "corrective crying" have you
punished a child for lying or telling a fib.
when you reach a certain stage in life
it's called an ad-lib.

It used to be synonymous with a politician's objective.
Avoid any questions and answer with deflection.
If you don't like the results just wait for the next election
In the meantime, no one truly answered the question.
We're no closer to the truth,
than from the previous election

Correction.
there was interference that went with objection.
Redacted answers as a reflection, question?
How many terrible paintings have you hung on the wall?
Do you tell a child they have no talent at all?
We lie when we feel it applicable,
when pain is too strong to grapple with

But to lie to keep what you lied to reap.
That's a lie that will take bodies six feet deep.
I repeat; that's a lie that will take bodies six feet deep.
Now I lay me down to sleep, one hell of a line
if you don't believe, I don't believe that some believe.
Praise god in the rising, but tonight we thieve.
Are we closer to the truth if we don't search for it?

DO I DO THAT?

I had to ask myself (which I often do) how racist am I?
Do I read a name and assume the origin of the person
if someone said that they were African American
does that fact become assumption just because
we've been taught the lines of demarcations?
Throughout our historical guffaws'.
Yeah, that life seemed funny to some
the opposite side of pain, is like money to some.
But do I do that? Do I assume black or pray that it's not.
when the news says something went down
"OH LORD don't let them be" Yeah, I know I do it.
I've done it, my reason for it my not be the same?

But it's the same,
shame it has to be that way
blame,
there's enough to circle the universe I'd say.
Human nature is human nature.
Just as day turns to night.
Have you turned down love simply because of perception?
Deep reflection,
choice is one thing I mean they are limitless.
Men and Women period
Let's just say there's a myriad
am I stuck at the base of the pyramid!
Should I question the origin of my lesson
and lesson the beauty of what I fear to attain?
What would my peers think?

hülya
n.
yılmaz

Professor Emerita (Humanities, Penn State, USA), hülya n. yılmaz [sic] is a published tri-lingual author, literary translator, and Director of Editing Services (Inner Child Press International, USA). Her work has appeared in numerous anthologies of global endeavors and was presented at poetry events in the U.S. and abroad. In 2018, the WIN of British Colombia, Canada honored yılmaz with a literary excellence award. Her two poems remain permanently installed in *Telepoem Booth* (USA). hülya finds it vital for everyone to understand a deeper sense of self, and writes creatively to attain a comprehensive awareness for and development of our humanity.

Writing Web Site
https://hulyanyilmaz.com/

Editing Web Site
https://hulyasfreelancing.com

Stop Telling . . .

Sit with your legs crossed in your mini skirt.

Show little to no skin in whatever you wear outside.

Don't laugh too much in public.

Have always a balanced meal ready for your husband.

Set your table elegantly.

Choose colors in a variety.

Presentation is, after all, an eye candy.

But no matter what you do,

don't ever be an eye candy.

Women to . . .

Why become a journalist?

You'll end up mixing with men.

Why study archeology?

Site visits will take you away from your family.

Why train as a simultaneous translator?

Can you not see?

A career in the parliament of your country

where it's the men who dominate key offices primarily

is not for a place for a woman to be.

Smile!

Feeling down?
Give us a smile!
Physically exhausted?
Give us a smile!
Mentally drained?
Give us a smile!
Emotionally worn?
Give us a smile!
Torn inside?
Smile!
Just smile!

Come on, try it one more time!

Now, was that so difficult?

hülya n. yılmaz

Teresa
E.
Gallion

Teresa E. Gallion

Teresa E. Gallion was born in Shreveport, Louisiana and moved to Illinois at the age of 15. She completed her undergraduate training at the University of Illinois Chicago and received her master's degree in Psychology from Bowling Green State University in Ohio. She retired from New Mexico state government in 2012.

She moved to New Mexico in 1987. While writing sporadically for many years, in 1998 she started reading her work in the local Albuquerque poetry community. She has been a featured reader at local coffee houses, bookstores, art galleries, museums, libraries, Outpost Performance Space, the Route 66 Festival in 2001 and the State of Oklahoma's Poetry Festival in Cheyenne, Oklahoma in 2004. She occasionally hosts an open mic.

Teresa's work is published in numerous Journals and anthologies. She has two CDs: *On the Wings of the Wind* and *Poems from Chasing Light*. She has published three books: *Walking Sacred Ground, Contemplation in the High Desert* and *Chasing Light.*

Chasing Light was a finalist in the 2013 New Mexico/Arizona Book Awards.

The surreal high desert landscape and her personal spiritual journey influence the writing of this Albuquerque poet. When she is not writing, she is committed to hiking the enchanted landscapes of New Mexico. You may preview her work at

http://bit.ly/1aIVPNq or *http://bit.ly/13IMLGh*

I Am Woman

I am woman,
strong, independent and free.
Do not tell me to smile.
Perhaps I am soaking in
a bad moment or bad day
that turns my lip upside down.

Perhaps I am hurting from
the abuse against my face.
Perhaps the smile will hurt
instead of relieve.

Perhaps I am tired from
smiling all day at rudeness,
arrogance and inconsiderateness.
My jaws may need a rest.

Perhaps you stepped on my foot and
forced your way into my space.
Perhaps I am in deep contemplation
that draws me inward
and my body surrenders to relaxation.

Perhaps I simply do not want to smile.
And by the way, I do not appreciate
you telling me what to do.

I am woman,
strong, independent and able
to do what pleases me quite well.

Ready to Hold You

My soul waits patiently
for your home coming.
The eternal love flame
still burns, lights the entrance
to my heart.

The love garden blooms
every year just for you.
All my senses awaken
with excitement
knowing you will see
the garden planted for you.

After many seasons' blooms,
we shall unite in passion
next to a red rose that bares
your name.

I stand with anticipation
at the garden gate,
heart in my hands.
ready to surrender to you.

She Speaks Through My Shoulder

I had a deep conversation with my shoulder.
She said, I got your attention with a rough blow.
Will you ever learn without the need
to be slapped so hard?

I could have left you in that ditch.
Chew on that until you are able
to digest my range of power.

You waited four weeks to start
the healing process.
Now you have six weeks
for constructive changes
in your behavior.

I will not ask you the question
until you repent for six months.
Do you know the question?
Yes, I said respectfully.
Did you learn the lesson?

Ashok K. Bhargava

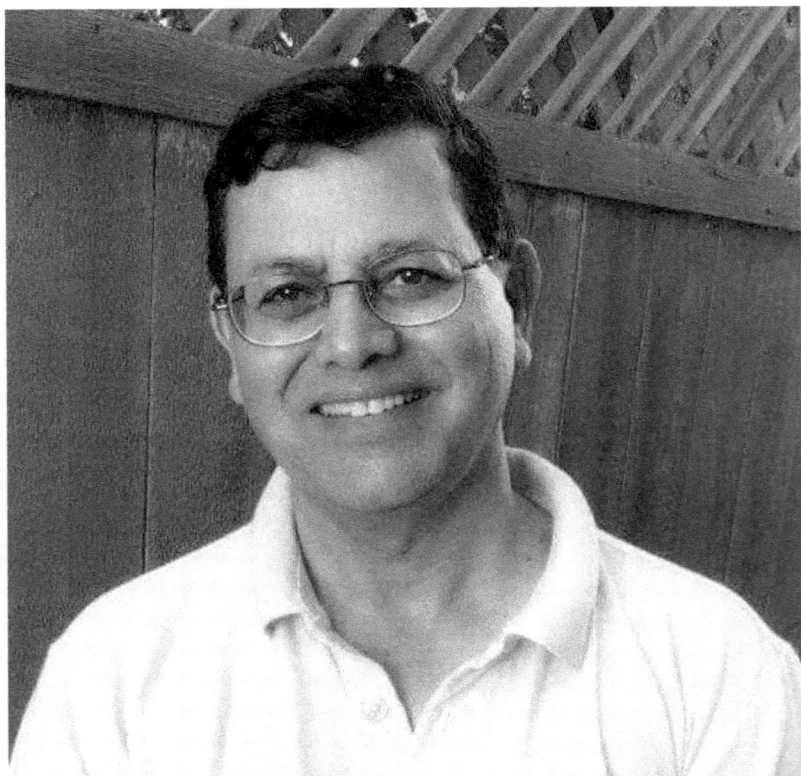

Ashok Bhargava is a poet, writer, community activist, public speaker, management consultant and a keen photographer. Based in Vancouver, he has published several collections of his poems: Riding the Tide, Mirror of Dreams, A Kernel of Truth, Skipping Stones, Half Open Door and Lost in the Morning Calm. His poetry has been published in various literary magazines and anthologies.

Ashok is a Poet Laureate and poet ambassador to Japan, Korea and India. He is founder of WIN: Writers International Network Canada. Its main objective is to inspire, encourage, promote and recognize writers of diverse genres, artists and community leaders. He has received many accolades including Nehru Humanitarian Award for his leadership of Writers International Network Canada, Poets without Borders Peace Award for his journeys across the globe to celebrate peace and to create alliances with poets, and Kalidasa Award for creative writings.

Me Remain Myself

Don't tell me
to become someone
that I am not.

I know
red roses and chocolates
are merely baits
to hook my soul
when words dissipate
without giving any options.

Don't ask me to smile and
dance to your whims.

My mind is a garden
I can dance with flowers
and taste the nectar
my power
remains intact
within me
when I'm myself.

Siege

Defiant flowers bloom
in unlikely places
layered folds of hair.

Eyes focused
at wisps
seeds on a page
connect to the joy of
written word.

A brick-wall wont's succeed
in separating me from
an epiphany
that love too undergoes
a gradual change.

Seeding

you follow the rising light
in the eastern sky
presaging
transience of darkness

realize that you are not
another brick in the wall
trying
to pull away

look at the garden that rises
from within
roots deep
inside the mind

soon birds would be drawn
prayers answered
darkness turn into
light

Caroline
'Ceri Naz'
Nazareno
Gabis

Carolin 'Ceri' Nazareno-Gabis

Caroline 'Ceri Naz' Nazareno-Gabis, author of Velvet Passions of Calibrated Quarks, World Poetry Canada International Director to Philippines is known as a 'poet of peace and friendship', a multi-awarded poet, editor, journalist, speaker, linguist, educator, peace and women's advocate. She believes that learning other's language and culture is a doorway to wisdom.

Among her poetic belts include PANORAMA YOUTH LITERARY AWARDS 2020, 7 th Prize Winner in the 19th, 20th and 21st Italian Award of Literary Festival; Writers International Network-Canada "Amazing Poet 2015", The Frang Bardhi Literary Prize 2014 (Albania), the sair-gazeteci or Poet Journalist Award 2014 (Tuzla, Istanbul, Turkey) and World Poetry Empowered Poet 2013 (Vancouver, Canada). She's a featured member of Association of Women's Rights and Development (AWID), The Poetry Posse, Galaktika Poetike, Asia Pacific Writers and Translators (APWT), Axlepino and Anacbanua.

Her poetry and children's stories have been featured in different anthologies and magazines worldwide.

Links to her works:

panitikan.ph/2018/03/30/caroline-nazareno-gabis

apwriters.org/author/ceri_naz/

www.aveviajera.org/nacionesunidasdelasletras/id1181 .html

Orenda

Mystical garden

In Gaia's face

Ceaseless energy cascading

Intangible waves

Of awakened soul,

Reverberate in the books

Of psalms

And borrowed tomorrows,

After you're gone.

from yesterday to here now

what's gone is not the ash
of yesterday's impulses
call it once, twice or even thrice of repeated
frequency of unexpected highs and low of lows
in the premises of unmistakable truths
completes the existence, in this four topsy turvy walls
wanting winner's wands to get inside fortune gates,
there are prompt approvals, sometimes set to wait
listen to the sound of emptiness…
how it flows to the chants of tasteless chords
how it burns the unwanted words
how it goes to the channels of adversities
here now, spread the wings of strength.

I do, but I also don't

i don't seek majesty
i don't like hypocrisy
i don't mind you choosing freedom
of thought, expression and speech lavishly
i don't want to be jailed
into misunderstanding,
hatred,
pride,
and lost of respect.

i don't have eyes, nose and mouth
to classify and separate
and push divisiveness.

i do make little things
to be my own riches
i do take simplicity at its best
to share it to the fullest.
i do listen.
i do care.
i do have open arms.
i do love each and everyone.

where is love, where is peace?
when you desire to tear all the pieces
take the courage to be--- a BETTER ONE.

Swapna Behera

Swapna Behera is a bilingual contemporary poet, author, translator and editor from Odisha, India. She was a teacher from 1984 to 2015. Her stories, poems and articles are widely published in National and International journals, and ezines, and are translated into different national and International languages. She has penned six books. She is the recipient of the Prestigious International Mother Language UGADI AWARD WINNER 2019. She was conferred upon the Prestigious International Poesis Award of Honor at the 2nd Bharat Award for Literature as Jury in 2015, The Enchanting Muse Award in India World Poetree Festival 2017, World Icon of Peace Award in 2017, and the Pentasi B World Fellow Poet in 2017. She is the recipient of the Prolific Poetess Award ,The Life time Achievement Award ,The Best Planner Award ,The Sahitya Shiromani Award, ATAL BIHARI BAJPAYEE Award, ATAL Award 2018 ,Global Literature Guardian Award ,International Life Time Achievement Award and the Master of Creative Impulse Award .She has received the Honoured Poet of India from the Seychelles Government accredited Literary Society Lasher one poem A NIGHT IN THE REFUGEE CAMP is translated into 60 languages .She is the Ambassador of Humanity by Hafrikan Prince Art World Africa 2018 and an official member of World Nation's Writers Union ,Kazakhstan2018. Italy, the National President for India by Hispanomundial Union of Writers (UHE), Peru, the administrator of several poetic groups, and the Cultural Ambassador for India and South Asia of Inner Child Press African is the life member of Odisha Environmental Society.

swapna.behera@gmail.com

stop telling

stop
racial injustice
stop telling women to smile
how illogical is the man-made ethics
stop says she
she is the art consultant
raised an artistic crusade against street harassers
brush and paint were her weapon
an oil painter was she
stop
"i am not here for you"
harassing women is not allowed
women are not for entertainment
She a visual artist TATYANA
who experiments, raises voice against racialism
series of portraits she made
"no, you can't talk to me for a minute"
the freedom of speech, rejection, liberty to live
let the woman live in a dignified way
safety. security the basic priority
a strong crusader, a feminist
whose arts speak aloud in million ways
women are not outside for entertainment
men command smile
they exhort
as though the faces are moulds
men can never demand, insist

eve teasing be abolished
let the women be happy
as a bird flying in the sky
for sky can never be a limit...

inside the shelf

near the super special hospital
under constriction
a temporary asbestos shed
the shelter of the labours of distant village
their clothes hang like the aerial roots of a Banyan tree
each one allotted with a plank-shelf
each worker's identity
his talisman
his tear and blood's document
in the shelf is a wrapped packet
the bangles of his wife
the migrant's better half
packed her love
in a red cloth
when he left his hut for work

the machine is screeching, pounding
the holocaust, trauma and stress
dust, sand and cement
dreams are whirling in the machine

the baby is moving round and round
in his wife's belly
millions of dreams crushed in the machine
after he gets the wage
he will rush to the village
gift a red saree to his wife
Can a machine understand the pain ever?
the mobile is ringing incessantly
message from his village

"the ambulance had no petrol
so, the patient died half away"
red bangles broken in the shelf
the scream tears
the concrete hospital
his wife's motionless body on the ground
now the foetus burning in the pyre with the mother
the shelf speaks history of a super special hospital
and
story of two drops of tears!

at last they reached

at last they reached
to a circle of their own
when they listened to their leader
they stamped on the dot
of a ballot

at last they poured oil to their lamps
woke up whole night to receive wisdom.
at last they reached the goal
their girls went to the school
 bicycles ran on the roads
illuminated versions started a road March

at last the cosy cuisine of love
was served on every plate
the city remembered
the culture of indigenous ancients.
skills preserved.
the listeners sat in every family
granny, the love guru of the family told stories

at last they spoke less, listened more ....
and destination peeped.
where water was saved
at last the swan crossed the traffic
at last, the aftermath was over
at last the migration was over
nature smiled ....
a pulsating secured zone marched forward ....

Albert
'Infinite'
Carrasco

Albert "Infinite The Poet" Carrasco is an urban poet, mentor and public speaker.

Albert believes his experience of growing up in poverty, dealing with drugs and witnessing murder over and over were lessons learnt, in order to gain knowledge to teach. Albert's harsh reality and honesty is a powerfully packed punch delivered through rhyme. Infinite grew up in the east part of the Bronx and still resides there, so he knows many young men will follow the same dark path he followed looking for change. The life of crime should never be an option to being poor but it is, very often.

Infinite poetry @lulu.com

Alcarrasco2 on YouTube

Infinite the poet on reverbnation

Infinite Poetry

http://www.lulu.com/us/en/shop/al-infinite-carrasco/infinite-poetry/paperback/product-21040240.html

March's picture prompt piece

She is so focused.
R.I.F. Reading is fundamental,
I can see she's getting her mental nourished.
Food for thought.
I see growth in the pursuit for intelligence,
Fiction or non fiction diction doesn't matter,
What matters is she's expanding her vocabulary in any instance.
Those eyes.
I wonder if she is reading history, separating truth from lies?
I wonder if she's looking at our ancestors and why they cry?
I wonder if she's trying to find a way to strengthen community ties?
Kids nowadays are addicted to social media and games,
I don't think this is this young lady's aim.
I think that her studies of organized letters will make our future brighter.
She's studying to be a Doctor, a Lawyer, a Teacher,
or maybe she'll be the next Kamala Harris, a leader.
knowledge is power.
Everything is possible when you're an avid reader.

I rolled with the best of them

I rolled with the best of them, moved packs with prospects and legends, didn't have a run, was active in war, did tours, infs a veteran. I was recruited by poverty and stationed in housing authority. concrete and wood trenches, red brick surrounded by wood benches, gates and fences worked in our favor because it would slow down the offensives while shown what defense is. Some pitched, grew, blew and became an underboss, others met the agony of defeat and got crucified where avenues and streets cross. The "game" is not a game, my dudes in Valhalla, St. Raymond's and Woodlawn would've respawned, my homie doing life and others doing football numbers would've been home with their kids, girls, wives and mothers... but there's no fuckn restarts or do overs. It's is what it is, I can't change consequence, I lived thru it, learnt from it, now it's gained experience. The game was a way to bring us up when we was down, then it was a race for the throne and everybody wanted that crown, dudes went here, went there, shit got real now there's hardly no one around, if they're not dead they're up for alleged blood shed, only a few abscond.

She sang

She used to sing to me, it would melt my heart, Every time I hear old melodies my mind goes into throw back mode and reminiscing starts. It was love. She made the thug in me all mushy, I stood there soakingin her voice silently as an audience of one listening to angelic acoustics. She could just move her mouth without sound and I'll be able to hear our favorite songs by reading her lips. She would always have me passionately paralyzed. looking into her eyes I'll instantly go under hypnosis, she's a problem, all It took was one kiss for me to know I'll be love sick, that was my immediate prognosis. Her touch was another thing, I'll get goose bumps all over when this queen grabs my hand as she sings for her King. It was love. What happened to we? I never thought our love would turn into an oldie but goodie

Eliza Segiet

Eliza Segiet: Master's Degree in Philosophy, completed postgraduate studies in Cultural Knowledge, Philosophy, Arts and Literature at Jagiellonian University. She is a member of The Association of Polish Writers and The NWNU - Union of Writers of the World.

Her poems *Questions* and *Sea of Mists* won the title of the International Publication of the Year 2017 and 2018 in Spillwords Press.

For her volume of *Magnetic People* she won a literary award of a *Golden Rose* named after Jaroslaw Zielinski (Poland 2019 r.). Her poem The *Sea of Mists* was chosen as one of the best one hundred poems of 2018 by International Poetry Press Publication Canada.

In Poet's Yearbook, as the author of *Sea of Mists*, she was awarded with the prestigious Elite Writer's Status Award as one of the best poets of 2019 (July 2019).

She was awarded *World Poetic Star Award* by World Nations Writers Union – the world's largest Writers' Union from Kazakhstan (August 2019).

In September 2019 she was 1st Place Laureate (Foreign Poetry category) – in Contest *Quando È la Vita ad Invitare* for poem *Be Yourself* (Italy).

Her poem *Order* from volume *Unpaired* was selected as one of the 100 best poems of 2019 in International Poetry Press Publications (Canada).

Nominated for the Pushcart Prize 2019.

Nominated for the iWoman Global Awards (2019).

Laureate Naji Naaman Literary Prize 2020.

Laureate International Award PARAGON OF HOPE (Canada, 2020).

Obtained certificate of appreciation from *Gujarat Sahitya Academy* and *Motivational Strips* for literary excellence par with global standards (2020).

Ambassador of Literature granted by *Motivational Strips*.

Author's works can be found in anthologies, separate books and literary magazines worldwide.

Power of Wisdom
To Tatyana Fazlalizadeh

Gender nor skin color
can't be igniters of aggression
Experiencing the world,
without torment from anyone,
is a human right.
When being broken
must through power of wisdom
fight the lack of understanding.

Defensive force
doesn't come from the void
because
the body's color is but a hull.
Inside it live
memories, plans,
dignity,
which must not be taken away

Translated by Ula de B.

Painted Lips

At the gate,
on the atoll of happiness
with lips
painted in a smile,
sits
Youth.

In a closed space
of its own pleasure,
it quietly departs.

Although power and impotence
is always with it,
it loses priceless time
life.

Translated by Artur Komoter

Pedestal

After all
like the moon
you can shine with reflected light.
However, it's better to have your own
power.

To be the brightness or the reflection?

To be yourself?
Or maybe a pedestal?

No shadows have monuments erected.

They disappear.

Translated by Artur Komoter

William S. Peters Sr.

Bill's writing career spans a period of over 50 years. Being first Published in 1972, Bill has since went on to Author in excess of 50 additional Volumes of Poetry, Short Stories, etc., expressing his thoughts on matters of the Heart, Spirit, Consciousness and Humanity. His primary focus is that of Love, Peace and Understanding!

Bill says . . .

I have always likened Life to that of a Garden. So, for me, Life is simply about the Seeds we Sow and Nourish. All things we "Think and Do", will "Be" Cause and eventually manifest itself to being an "Effect" within our own personal "Existences" and "Experiences" . . . whether it be Fruit, Flowers, Weeds or Barren Landscapes! Bill highly regards the Fruits of his Labor and wishes that everyone would thus go on to plant "Lovely" Seeds on "Good Ground" in their own Gardens of Life!

to connect with Bill, he is all things Inner Child

www.iaminnerchild.com

Personal Web Site

www.iamjustbill.com

Reading is Fundamental

I shall honor my ancestors,
Yes, I shall,
For they fought for me,
They suffered for me,
They marched for me,
They died for me,
To have this right,
To read

You see,
Reading was forbidden,
For in words found
Here and there
Between the covers
Of books and such
There was much
To be learned

My mind shall blossom,
And flowers and fruit
Shall grow abundantly,
And I will have planted the seeds
That I will pass on,
For some day,
I too will become
An ancestor,
And my children,
Your children
Will prosper,
As shall the world
Of us all

Reading is Fundamental

Old Toys

No one particularly cares for
Old Toys ...
Except . . .
Those who have none,
Or collectors,
Or those who dwell in the
'I remember when's ...'

Yes, for most,
Things were simpler
Back then,
And the generations to come,
Are doomed
To think pretty much
The same way

Bicycles had 1 gear,
And my first had no
Training wheels,
And of course,
I was enthralled with excitement,
When I got my 1st 3 speed,
Then there was 5 speeds,
Then 10,
And now
You can have
As many as you want
.....
Just pedal my friend,
Just pedal

From simple things
Where people engaged

With people,
With few props needed,
To now,
Where everything requires
Batteries or electricity
.....
Recharge !!!! . . .
Yes recharge your delusions,
For the illusion
Of being sated,
Satisfied,
Content,
Requires more energy
Than we have to give,

Throwing stones,
Hopscotch,
Racing,
Jumping rope,
Climbing trees,
Ring-around-the-rosey,
Hide & Seek ....
Who does that anymore?

And then there were . . .
Rocking Horses,
Jacks,
Jack-in-the-box,
Dolls,
Playing House,
Skates and Scooters and Milk Crates,
Building Blocks and Wagons,
Clay for Play and Play Doh
Oh, Oh, Oh,
And so much more

That required me/us/we
To be there
Mentally . . .
. . . .

Where's my tablet?,
Where's my phone,
I need to get on the internet,
"Mom, there is something wrong
With the WiFi" . .
OMG (Oh My God)
The Sky is falling !!!!!

Let's Skype, let's Zoom,
While Google
Plays and Talks ....
We can Live-Stream
On FaceBook, Google or YouTube,
See you there,
Don't be late,
It'll be a blast

Many dwell,
Or get stuck
In the past ....
Been there, done that,
And I may do it again,
For the territory,
Is obligatory
To my angst,
And my need to escape

The imagination
That once occupied
Our idle time,
Our play times

Has somehow slipped away,
Or abandoned us,
And we forgot how to see ourselves
As heroes of the day ....
Super you say man,
Woman,
As the 'band of farce-ness' plays
Its discordant tune ....

A fine mess
Rules our days
Our ways,
As we seek to play
With 'Old Toys'

Come on Girls and Boys,
Let's act like children . . . again
.....
Where is my sanity?

Not Quite

Nostalgic tears
From a yesterday gone
Flowing in my soul
Reminding everyone
Of bruises suffered
By this heart of mine

Yes, I have become stronger,
But at what cost
Do I claim
Those seemingly empty victories
Over my pain

It seems to me
That these days and times
Are acute reminders
That time has not moved,
Only my focus,
And my consciousness
Have traversed that chasm
Where emptiness looms
And threatens
My conjured and put upon
Peace

I have learned
Quite aptly I must say The art-form
Of adorning my countenance
And my persona
In pretty and acceptable raiment,
Am not I comely too?
....

But I was not fooled
By these skewed shenanigans ....
Perhaps the world was,
But I succinctly knew
That was in need
Of mending,
For I was almost irreparably broken
By these same endurances
I convinced myself
I had to mitigate
That I may call myself
A man
....
All but another falsehood

So, here I am,
Wondering
If I am 'not quite' ready
For another go
At the illusions,
Hopefully this time
To rend the curtain,
Pierce the veil
That I may understand and experience
The meaning of liberation
From this 'self' of mine
I have claimed As my truth,
Or is this but another reckoning
Where again I am compelled
To acquiesce
To yet another 'Not Quite'?

March

2021

Featured Poets

~ * ~

Claudia Piccinno

Mohammed Jabr

Luzviminda Rivera

Nigar Arif

i Fly
because ... said the Dreamer to the world. I Can

Claudia Piccinno

Claudia Piccinno

Claudia Piccinno was born in the south of Italy, but she lives and teaches in the north of Italy . Operating in more than 100 anthologies, she's a former member of the jury in many national and international literary prizes. She is the Continental Director for Europe in the World Festival Poetry, she represents Istanbul culture in Italy as Ambassador of Ist Sanat Art Association.She has published 34 poetry books, among his own poetry collections and other poets' translation into italian language. She was conferred with the most prestigious award "Stele of Rosetta" in Istanbul in 2016, "World icon for peace" for Wip in Ondo city, Nigeria, on April 2017 ; Najiman prize in Liban on July 2018 and almost 250 prize in Italy for cultural merits. Her poem "In Blue" is played on a majolica stele posted on the seafront in Santa Caterina di Nardo (Le).

She is european editor for the international literary magazine Papirus in Turkey and for Atunis Magazine international. She is responsible for poetry in the italian magazine called Gazzetta di Istanbul, printed in Turkey by Italian community

Web Site

https://claudiapiccinno.weebly.-com/

Partire e ritornare

Dal cielo al mare
e dalla terra al cielo
con moto perpetuo e circolare,
sfido burrasche e venti
senza mai arretrare.
Sono piccola e flessibile,
mi adatto alle correnti,
volteggiare non so
come un fiocco di neve,
né tintinnare potrò
come un chicco di grandine.
Sono lo sfogo delle nuvole,
son la manna pei campi arati,
il desiderio dei passerotti
nella calura d'agosto.
Sono un pizzico di zanzara
per l'irato torrente,
sono una suora tra tante
nel placido fiume.
Lesta m'incammino
 verso il mare e lì io danzo
 tra le onde e gli scogli
per rarefarmi un giorno
e riabbracciare il cielo.
Partire e ritornare…
altro non saprei fare.

Leaving and coming back

From sky to sea
and from earth to heaven
with perpetual and circular motion
I challenge squalls and winds
and I never retreat.
I am small and flexible,
I adapt to the current
I can't twirl like a snowflake,
nor will I rattle like a hailstone.
I am the outburst of the clouds,
I am the manna through the plowed fields,
I am the desire of young sparrows
in the heat of August.
I am a mosquito's bite
for the angry stream,
I am a nun among other ones
in the placid river.
Deft I walk down to the sea
and there I dance
between the waves and the rocks
thinning myself one day
and embracing the sky.
Leaving and coming back
otherelse I couldn't do.

Mare nostrum

Ode a te culla liquida dei sognatori,
 "musa" di pittori e narratori,
"terra promessa"
pei gabbiani e i pescatori!
Ode a te
Specchio silente di ribelli e di pionieri,
"Caronte" pei gommoni di stranieri!
Turbato è il tuo frenetico pulsare
dalle scorie della centrale nucleare.
Ode alle risa spumeggianti dei bagnanti!
Ode al solletico che Grecale e Maestrale
saggian sull'innocenza dell'onda.
Mute e sorde sono le coscienze
degli impavidi timonieri notturni.
Ode a te, Mare Nostrum,
ode al tuo improvvisarti
pentagramma di coro a più voci,
cassa di risonanza di nenie veloci,
strada maestra della speranza,
monito vibrante a evitar la mattanza.

Mare Nostrum

Ode to you
liquid cradle for the dreamers,
Muse" for painters and for novelists,
 "Promised land"
for seagulls and fishermen!
Ode to you
silent mirror
 for rebels and for pioneers,
"Caronte"
for the inflatable boats of strangers
Disturbed is your frenetic pulsing
because of the dross of the nuclear power plant.
Ode to the sparkling laughters of bathers!
Ode to the tickle that Grecale and Maestrale
test on the innocence of the wave.
Deaf and mute are the consciences
of the brave nocturnal helmsmen
Ode to you, Mare Nostrum,
ode to your improvising yourself
pentagram of a several voices chorus,
sounding box of quick lullabies,
main road of hope,
vibrant warning to avoid the the mattanza.

Davide è il tuo nome
(dedicato a un bambino affetto d'autismo)

Dov'è fermo il tuo sguardo Davide?
Inciampasti nel dettaglio
per non vedere l'insieme.
Non è facile decifrare la bussola dei sensi
in tale marasma di stimoli sociali.
E come sosterrò io
la ricompensa di quella biologia molesta?
Rispettare la mancata connessione
tra le tue abilità sensoriali
è fatica immane per noi *così detti normali*.
Sopperire coi gesti a un'attenzione condivisa,
portarti a esplicitare una richiesta,
sono finalità impellenti nella mia testa.
Davide è il tuo nome,non sei per me diagnosi
né variante o falla di architettura genetica,
aspettativa disattesa, precoce o tardivo intervento,
compromessa plasticità cerebrale, disturbo dello spettro.
Davide è il tuo nome …
il bambino che ama il dettaglio. . .
Indosserò il tuo sguardo,
ascolterò la tua confusa stereotipia,
scenderò a incrociare l'oggetto che ti attrae
per accorciare la distanza
che ti tiene relegato in una stanza.

David is your name
Poem dedicated to a child with autism

Where did your gaze stop David?
You fell on a detail
in order not to see the whole.
It is not easy to decipher
the compass of the senses
in the chaos of social stimuli.
And how will Isupport the reward
of that troublesome biology ?
To observe the failure in the connection
among your sensory abilities
it is an enormous effort for us,
so-called normal.
To compensate with gestures
to a shared attention,
to take you to clarify a request,
They are compelling purposes in my head.
David is your name,
you're not for me a diagnoses
or variant or flaw of genetic architecture,
disregarded expectation,
early or late intervention,
impaired brain plasticity,
spectrum disorder.
David is your name
the child who loves the detail.
I'll wear your look,
I 'll listen to your confused stereotypy
I'll go down to cross the object that attracts you
to shorten the distance that keeps you confined in a room.

Il coraggio dei perdenti

Ha gli occhi grandi Ismael,
la bocca arsa Ikrahm,
voce squillante Aziz.
Sono lontani dal treno del vento,
dal kindertransport inglese
quando la guerra flagellava
l'Europa.
Sono i bambini in cammino
occhi innocenti di oggi,
agnelli di via crucis
per terra e per mare
quelli che vediamo sfilare al tg
noi servi di Caronte,
noi i "civili"
ostaggio dell'indifferenza,
vittime e forse complici
di tanta assuefazione.
Stiamo sul ciglio del sentiero
affollato di mani tese,
noi... stiamo immobili
col braccino nascosto
che non si scomponga
in offerte d'aiuto.
Ha gli occhi grandi Ismael,
la bocca arsa Ikrahm,
voce squillante Aziz.
Frastuono di bombe
nei loro ricordi,
piaghe ai piedi
e geloni alle mani.
Il manganello delle guardie
non risparmia nessuno,

è peggio dell'altalena delle maree,

sembra la fame dei pescecani.
Miseria, fame, epidemie.
Ismaèl, Ikrahm, Aziz;
partire, restare, tornare
la civile Europa ha inventato
un dispositivo micidiale:
il campo profughi
per farci assuefare
alla diaspora degli innocenti
all'ottusità delle nostre menti
al coraggio senza pari dei perdenti.

The courage of the losers

He has big eyes …Ismael
a parched mouth Ikrahm,
a ringing voice Aziz.
They are far from the train of the wind
the English Kindertransport
when the war afflicted Europe.
They are the kids on the way
The innocent eyes of today,
the lambs sacrified to the cross
by land and by sea
those we see parading at the tv news
we the servants of Charon,
we"the civilians"
we hostage of indifference,
victims and possibly accomplices
of a similar addiction..
We are on the edge of the path
crowded with outstretched hands,
we... we are motionless
with our hidden little arms
that do not essay to offer any help.
He has big eyes …Ismael
a parched mouth Ikrahm,
a ringing voice Aziz.
Din of bombs
in their memories,
at the foot sores
chilblains and hands.
The baton of the guards
spares no one,
It is worse than the swing of the tides,

It seems the hunger of sharks.
Poverty, famine, epidemics.
Ismael, Ikrahm, Aziz;
To go, to stay, to come back
The civilized Europe has invented
a deadly device:
the refugee camp
to make us accustom
to the diaspora of the Lambs
to the obtuseness of our minds
to the unmathed courage of the losers.

Claudia Piccinno

Claudia Piccinno

Mohammed
Jabr

Mohammed Jaber Ahmed is a poet and a civil society activist .born in Iraq, Mosul in 1978, he received a BA in Philosophy from University of Baghdad in 2004, his first collection of poetry (Creation Strewing) was published in 2012. he participated in supervising the preparation of a book (The Anthology of Contemporary Iraqi Poetry from 1981-2010) in both Arabic and English, with full funding from the Iraqi Ministry of Culture on the occasion of Baghdad as the Capital of Arab Culture in 2015, his second collection of poetry (Wards for Evidence of Love) it's won the Poet's Prize, haseb Sheikh Jaafar , he participated in the International Poetry Festival (Live Voices) in the French city of Sete 2017

The Most Beautiful is That …

One morning

As I opened the window,

God was before me.

So, I closed it up,

And then I opened it again

To have the whole of me in awe:

Oh, God!

There I caught the sight of a tree

moving fast among the seasons.

O, God, at last,

I could see

What's been yet invisible.

The windows went on opening and closing for me

Translated by Hussein Nasser Jabr

A Body by Chance

Streets, clinging to our bodies .. sticky,
Occult the dawn
By ads suffocating our colorful days .. with grief,
Portraying the showers of my hands on your glamorous
body
On streets .. white and wooded,
I Open a new page for your breasts
Floating in the air of love,
 To Shed me with light
Through an Asian bathhouse decorated with lather
And showers of rain trembling - drop by drop
tickling the mirror our images were sharing -
our sensual pictures, opposite to each other there-
Where rain was showering us with ecstasy
And forming as
Two who met in the street, by chance,
Each would go his way.

Translated by Hussein Nasser Jabr

The Apple and its Rib

Blood throbs in my hand
From your breath
And a rib, at the edge of the world
Is becoming green after the grass fades away
So that you come put: a woman
Sometimes, we bring philosophy together to complete the
missing rib
Of an apple that fell from you
And when we don't find time, the wound of music urge us
Like another fire, calming the flame
And my missing ribs
From
Which
Dream
Will you one day produce your legacy?

Translated by Safa Sheikh Hamad

Luzviminda Rivera

Luzviminda G. Rivera is a multi-awarded published author and excellent international research journal reviewer, multi-awarded researcher and world inspirational poet from the Philippines. She is also a multi-awarded nurse by profession, a fluent speaker of six languages. She is also a licensed teacher and finished her post graduates courses with an academic excellence award like the Doctor of Public Administration (6thdegree) and took up units leading to a Bachelor of Law. Her books were: A Gift and A Gift II available in Amazon and Crossroads: A Poet's Life Journey – an anthology. Currently, she is a moderator for the Philippines Office of the Motivational Strips and one (1) of the approving editors of Bharath Vision web magazine based in India.

In The End

In times like this…
What really matters ..
In the End..

In the end
Beauty will fade
Strength will perish
Success, recognition and fame will be irrelevant
Achievements will be useless
Degrees will no longer be counted
Beautiful places will fade
Wealth will disappear.

In the end
It is the inner beauty that counts
The strength you give for touching other lives
It is the significance of your success that will make you
relevant
It is the inspiration that you give that will make you shine
your brilliance
It is not what you learn but what have you become
It is the meaning of the places you leave your imprint
It is the value of compassion and good deeds
The true wealth that remains in the hearts.

In the end
It is your legacy of being competent
Character, compassion and integrity
that will be remembered by those who love and surround you
And…
It is between you and the LIVING GOD.
When you are finally gone
IN THE END.

Nothing Belong to Us

Nothing belongs to us
We are busy looking and working for
Money, wealth, fame and recognition
They all belong to EARTH.

Nothing belongs to us
We are busy filling our bucket list
Collecting memories from travel
They all belong to TIME.

Nothing belongs to us
We are busy honing our talents and gifts
Making innovation and making life easier
They all belong to CIRCUMSTANCES.

Nothing belongs to us
Working hard for the future of our families
Valuing friendships and camaraderie
They all belong to PATH.

Nothing belongs to us
We value our body so much
Investing so much money, time and effort
They all belong to DUST.

Nothing belongs to us
What we have is MOMENT.
Use that moment to do good
They all belong to God

Life is just a moment
Nothing belongs to us
Your cares, pride, and beauty
They all belong to the earth.

Life after death
Even our soul does not belong to us
Life of bliss and everlastingness
They all belong to God

A New Beginning

Every morning that brings new life
Is a new beginning:
To shine like the sunrise
To smell the aroma of fragrant flower
To feel the touch of the billowing breeze
To hear the rustling leaves of the trees
To see the refreshing view of clouds
To witness the vibrant colors of rainbows

Above all
A new beginning:

To treasure our moment on earth
To let go of the things that belong to the earth
To focus on what counts most
In the end

Nigar Arif

Nigar Arif

Nigar Arif was born in 1993 on 20th of January in Azerbaijan. She studied at Azerbaijan State Pedagogical University in the English faculty in 2010- 2014. Nigar Arif is a member of the "World Youth Turkish Writers' Union" and graduated from "III Youth Writers' School" in "Azerbaijan Writers' Union". She is also a member of the "International Forum for Creativity and Humanity" in Morocco. Her poems have been partially translated into English, Turkish, Russian, Persian, Montenegro, and Spanish and have been published in different countries. She was a participant of " IV LIFT- Eurasian Literary Festival of Festivals" which was held in Baku in 2019 and "30 Festival Internacional De Poesia De Medillin" in 2020 which was held in Colombia at online platform and at the 11th episode of "100 Poets around the World for Love" in the Gronthee Facebook Series. She participated at" Wordtrip Europe" project and " Fourth Global Poet Virtual Meeting 2020" as well.

The Wind

Hey wind, knocking door to door,
is that one door you're looking for,
is that enough for you?
Where are they now,
those open doors
from the hot, sunny days of summer?
Where are those that loved you,
to dine with and to rest;
who once were pleased to welcome you
and treat you as their guest?
Hey wind, knocking door to door,
where are your lovers now?
Now the weather's turned to winter,
have they turned cold as well?
Don't knock, my dear, don't knock,
no one's opening their door,
no one will look out for you, nor call on you,
no more.
Who, I ask, now the weathers changed,
would call on you at all?
Go dear, go.
Just wander round these dull grey streets
and break dry trees in anger;
just wait as winter turns to summer and your friends,
dear wind, with the sun, will grow again once more.

The clock is slow

Look at the world's clock
It's an hour slow.
Either joy is late,
Or life is drowned by sorrow.

Even if it talks and laughs
like a happy old man.
The world's laughs are lame
as the tired past.

He's begging or seeking
with a wishful hand.
And spends the days on steps
Fighting against the wind.

Out of the sweeper's eyes
Falling his nights.
The broom in the calloused hands
wakes up the sleepy streets.

He is a driver on the bus
Passenger in the wishes,
Looking for his fate
With the hope to change.

Look at the world's clock
It 's an hour slow.
Let's set up it anew,
For a better life than now.

The Reconciliation

Hey man, taking umbrage at himself,
Have you done a lot of sinning?
All you've lost, is just yourself,
Is there anything you gained?

Who took you from you?
Who left you to the void?
Who put his hand on your heart?
And calmed you like that?

Who ruined your life and fate
looking at your "sorry" face?
What did he leave in your eyes,
Dropping as tears?

Maybe it's you, and,
you've become a pain for yourself?
Maybe you just let your joys
slip through your fingers?

Hey you,
Who's oppressed by sorrow,
Walking in his thoughts,
Getting tired of his ways...
Losing the sun among complaints.

.

Turn back,
Make peace with yourself.
Shake hands and have faith ,
With that one whom you turned away

Remembering

our fallen soldiers of verse

Janet Perkins Caldwell

February 14, 1959 ~ September 20, 2016

Alan W. Jankowski

16 March 1961 ~ 10 March 2017

Now available

World Healing World Peace
2020

Poets for Humanity

Inner Child Press

News

Poetry Posse Members

We are so excited to share and announce a few of the current books, as well as the new and upcoming books of some of our Poetry Posse authors.

On the following pages we present to you ...

Jackie Davis Allen

Gail Weston Shazor

hülya n. yılmaz

Nizar Sartawi

Faleeha Hassan

Fahredin Shehu

Caroline 'Ceri' Nazareno

Eliza Segiet

Teresa E. Gallion

William S. Peters, Sr.

COMING SOON

www.innerchildpress.com

Eliza Segiet

To Be More

Inner Child Press News

Now Available at

www.innerchildpress.com

Scent of Love

Poetry by

Teresa E. Gallion

Now Available

www.innerchildpress.com

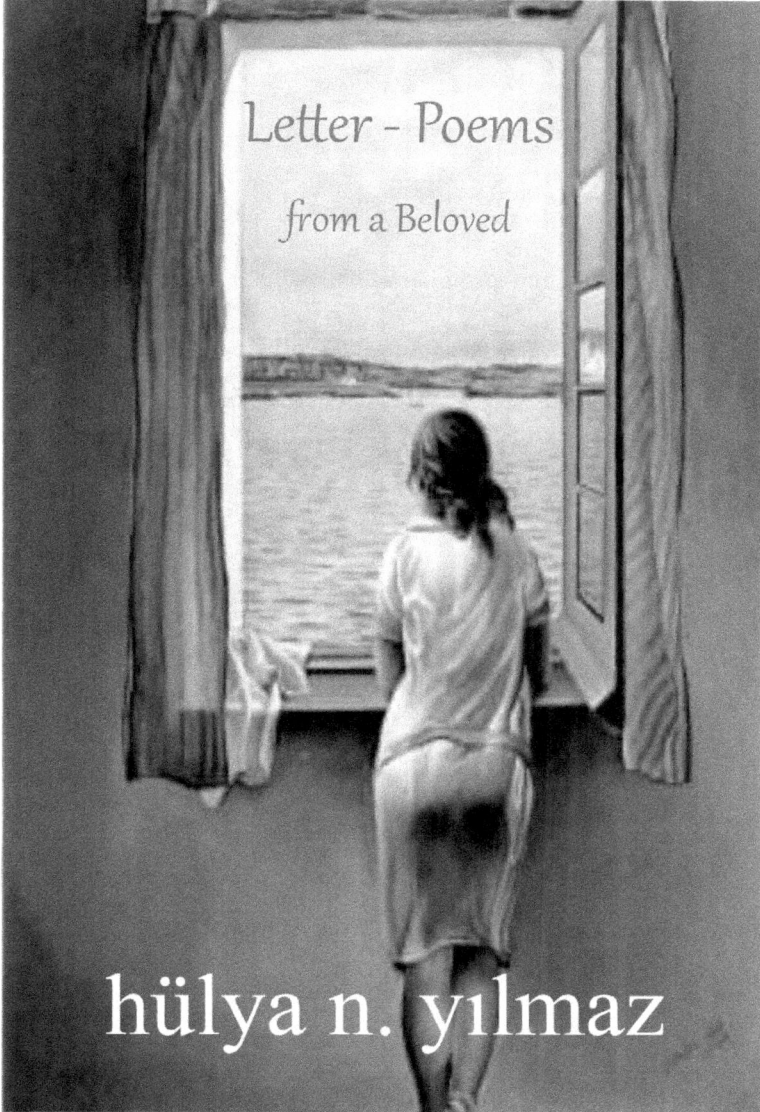

Letter - Poems

from a Beloved

hülya n. yılmaz

Now Available

www.innerchildpress.com

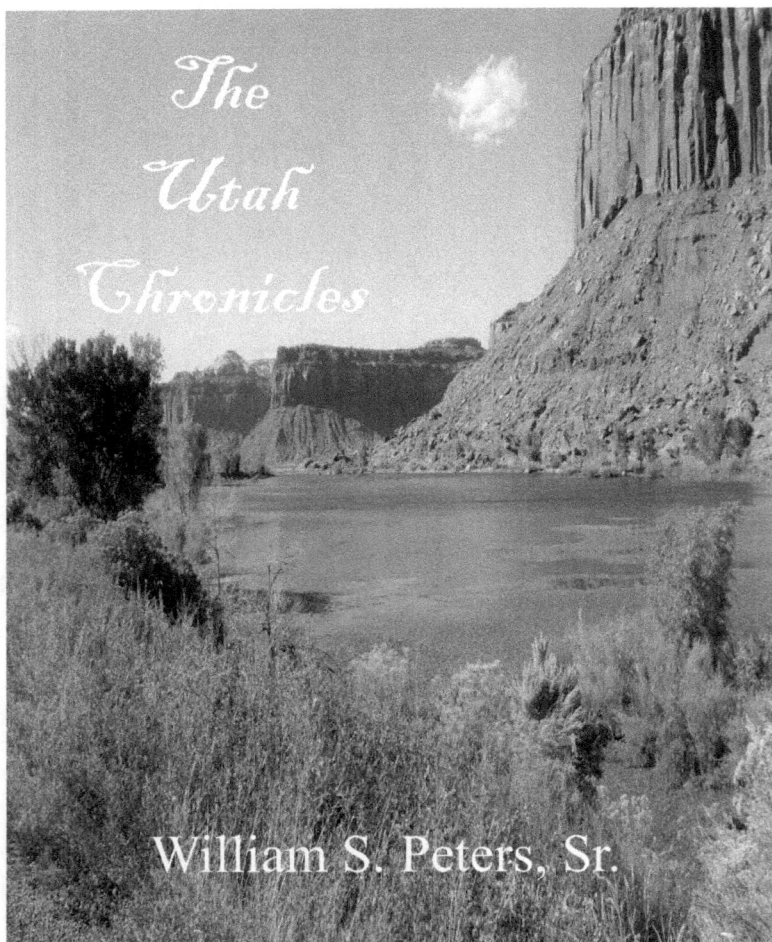

The
Utah
Chronicles

William S. Peters, Sr.

Now Available
www.innerchildpress.com

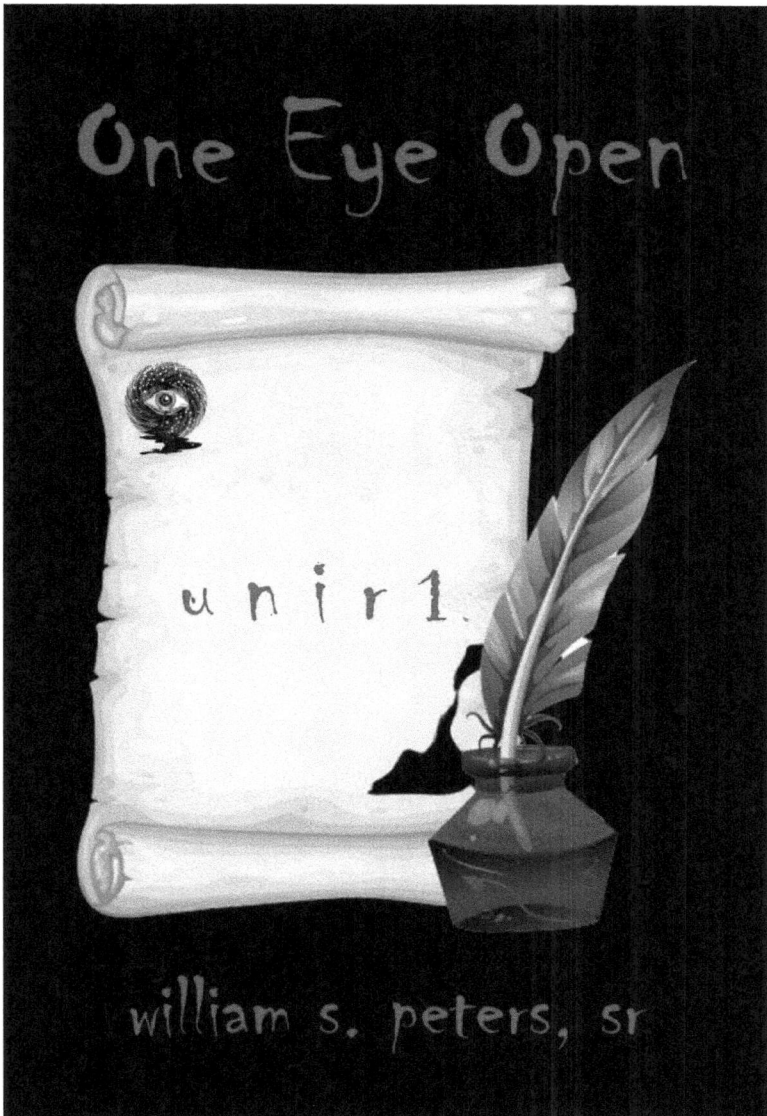

The Book of krisar

volume v

william s. peters, sr.

Now Available
www.innerchildpress.com

The Book of krisar

Volume I

william s. peters, sr.

The Book of krisar

Volume II

william s. peters, sr.

The Book of krisar

Volume III

william s. peters, sr.

The Book of krisar

Volume IV

william s. peters, sr.

Now Available
www.innerchildpress.com

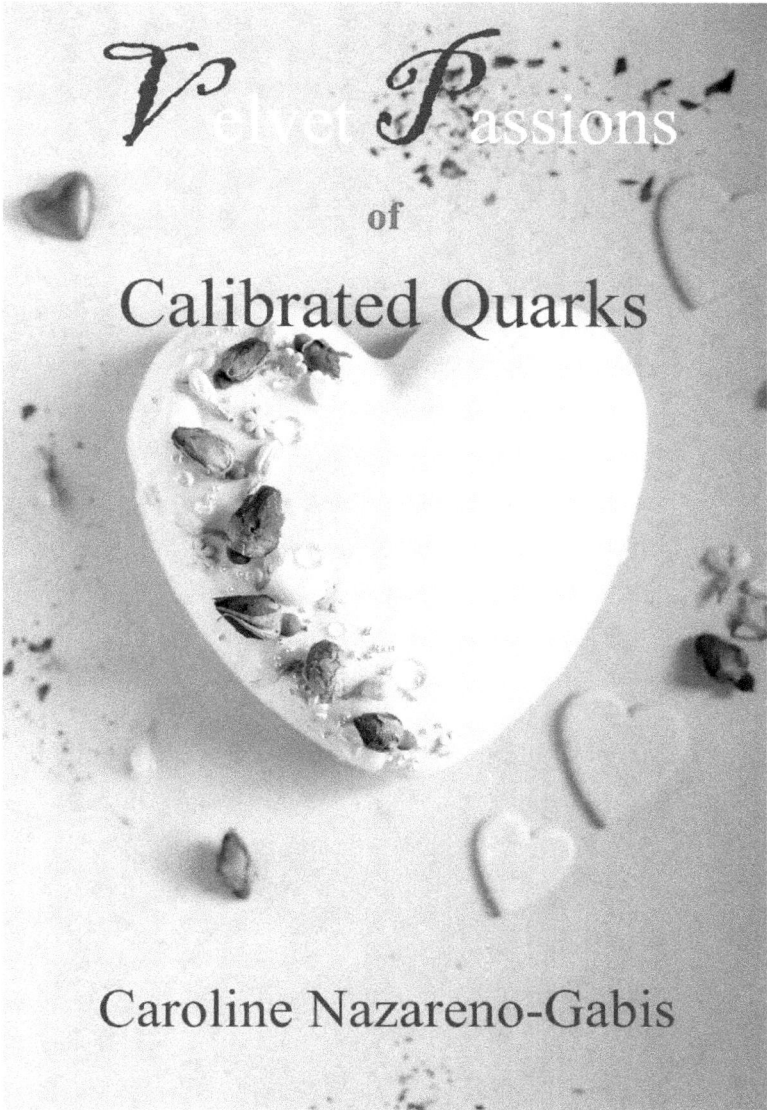

*V*elvet *P*assions

of

Calibrated Quarks

Caroline Nazareno-Gabis

Inner Child Press News

Now Available

www.innerchildpress.com

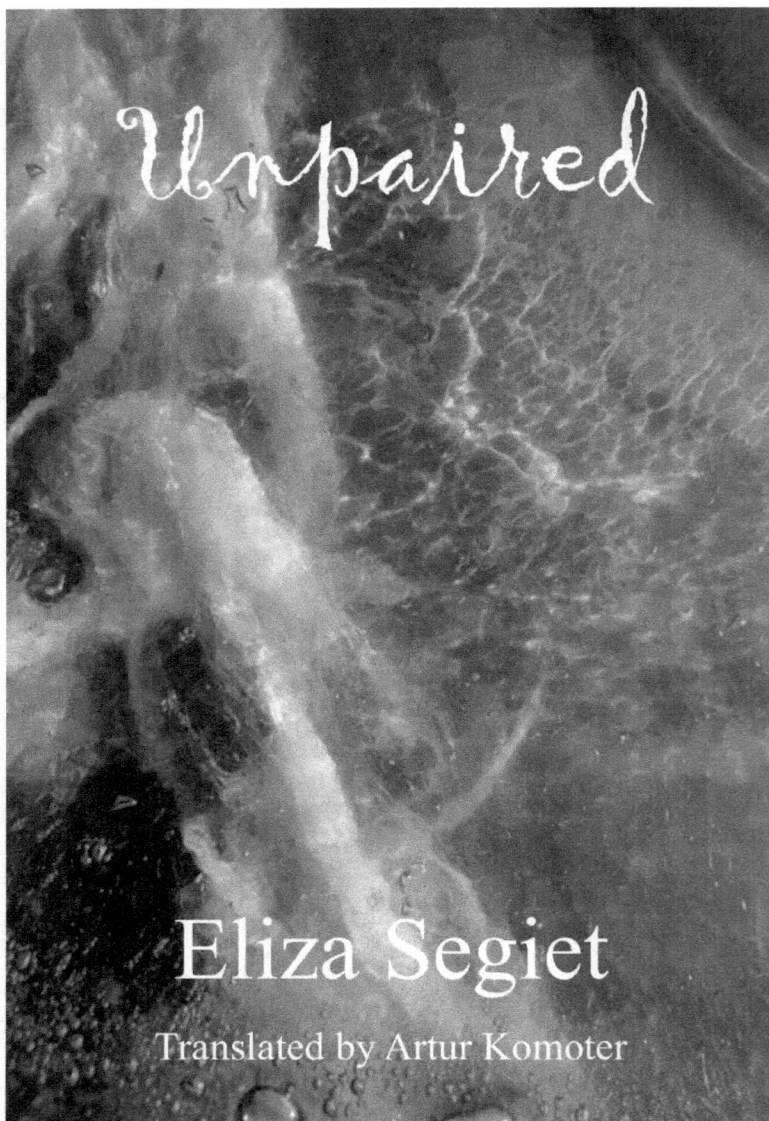

Unpaired

Eliza Segiet

Translated by Artur Komoter

Private Issue

www.innerchildpress.com

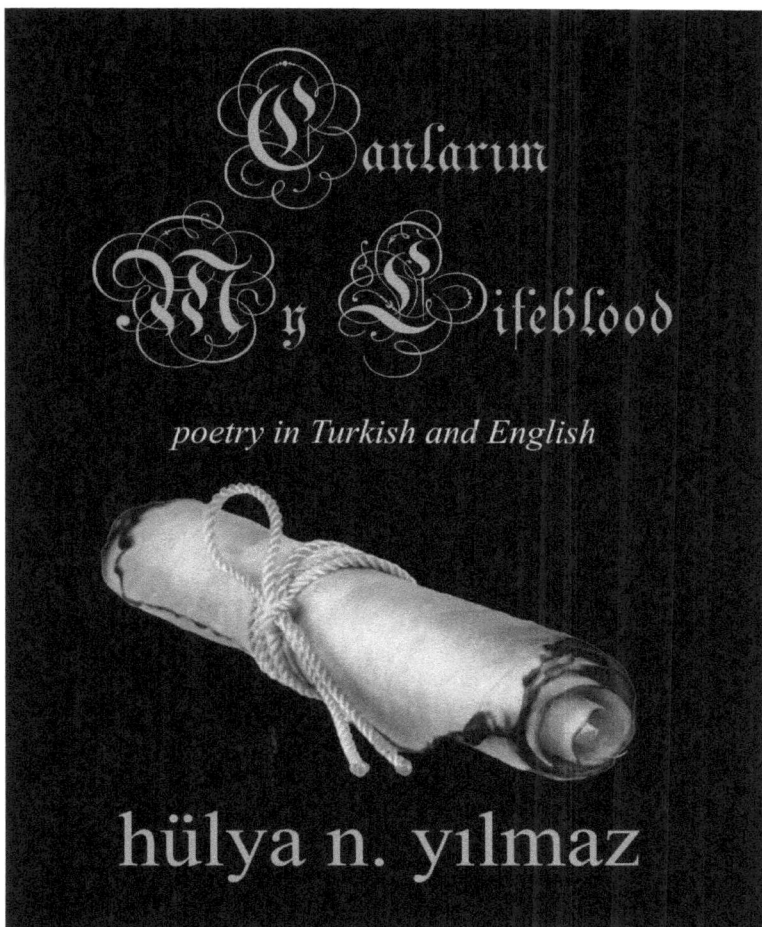

Canlarım

My Lifeblood

poetry in Turkish and English

hülya n. yılmaz

Now Available

www.innerchildpress.com

Butterfly's Voice

Faleeha Hassan

Translated by William M. Hutchins

Now Available at
www.innerchildpress.com

No Illusions

Through the Looking Glass

Jackie Davis Allen

Now Available at
www.innerchildpress.com

Now Available at

www.innerchildpress.com

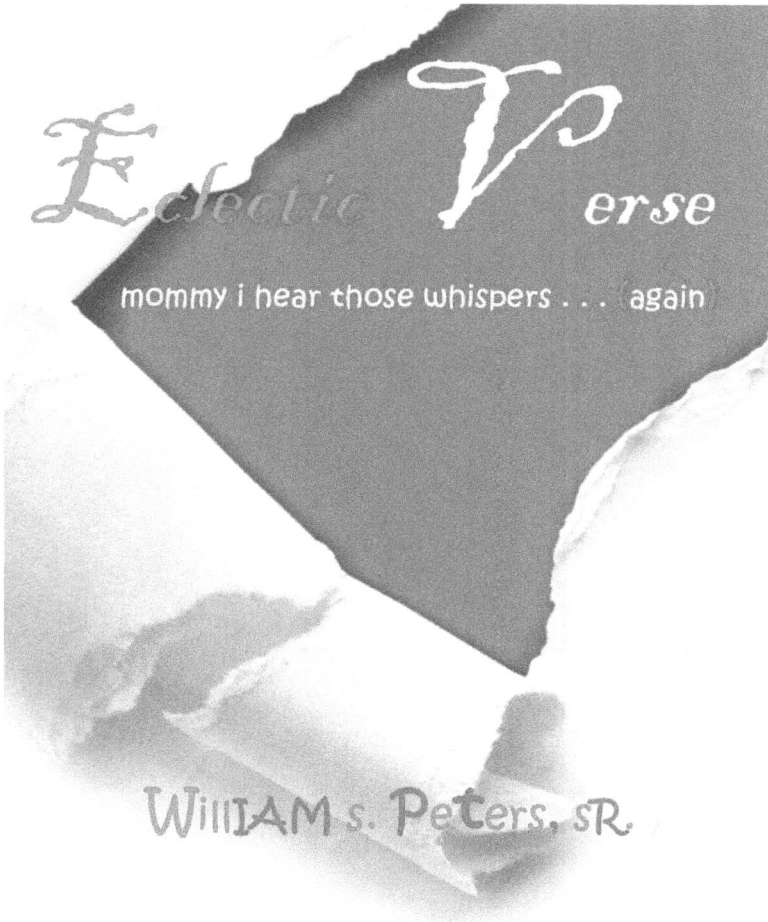

Eclectic Verse

mommy i hear those whispers . . . (again)

WilliAM s. PeTers, sR.

Inner Child Press News

Now Available at
www.innerchildpress.com

HERENOW

FAHREDIN SHEHU

Now Available at
www.innerchildpress.com

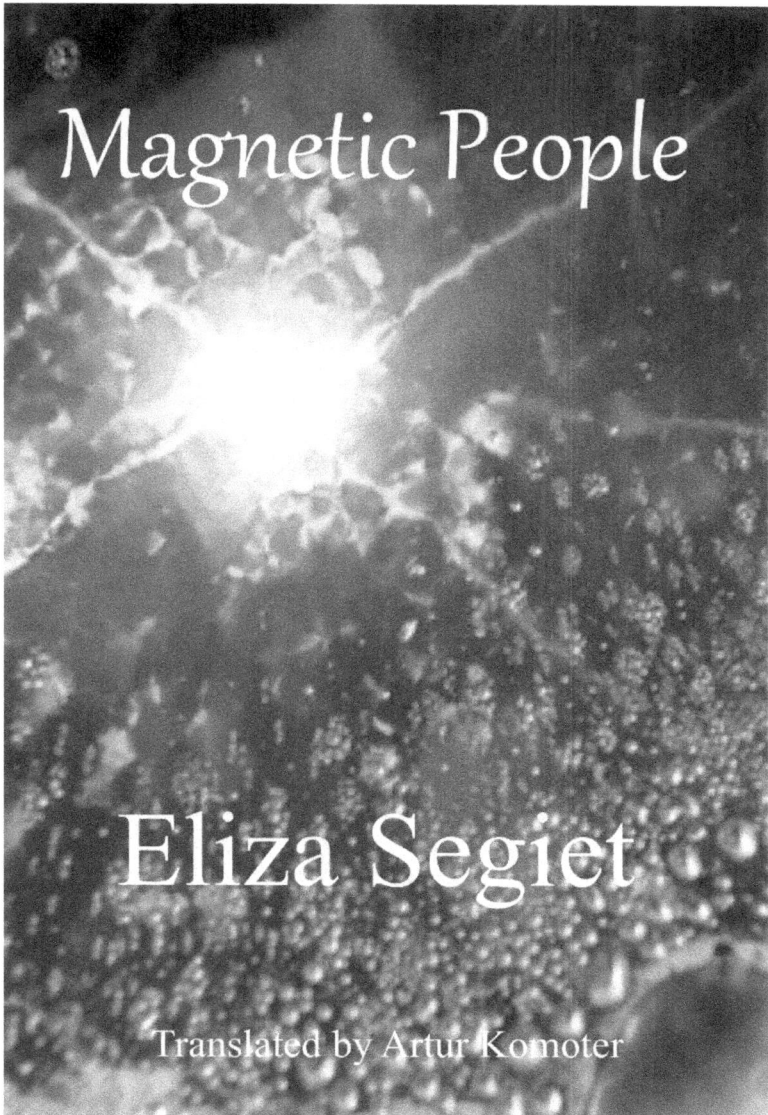

Magnetic People

Eliza Segiet

Translated by Artur Komoter

Now Available at
www.innerchildpress.com

Dark Side

of the

Moon

Jackie Davis Allen

Now Available at
www.innerchildpress.com

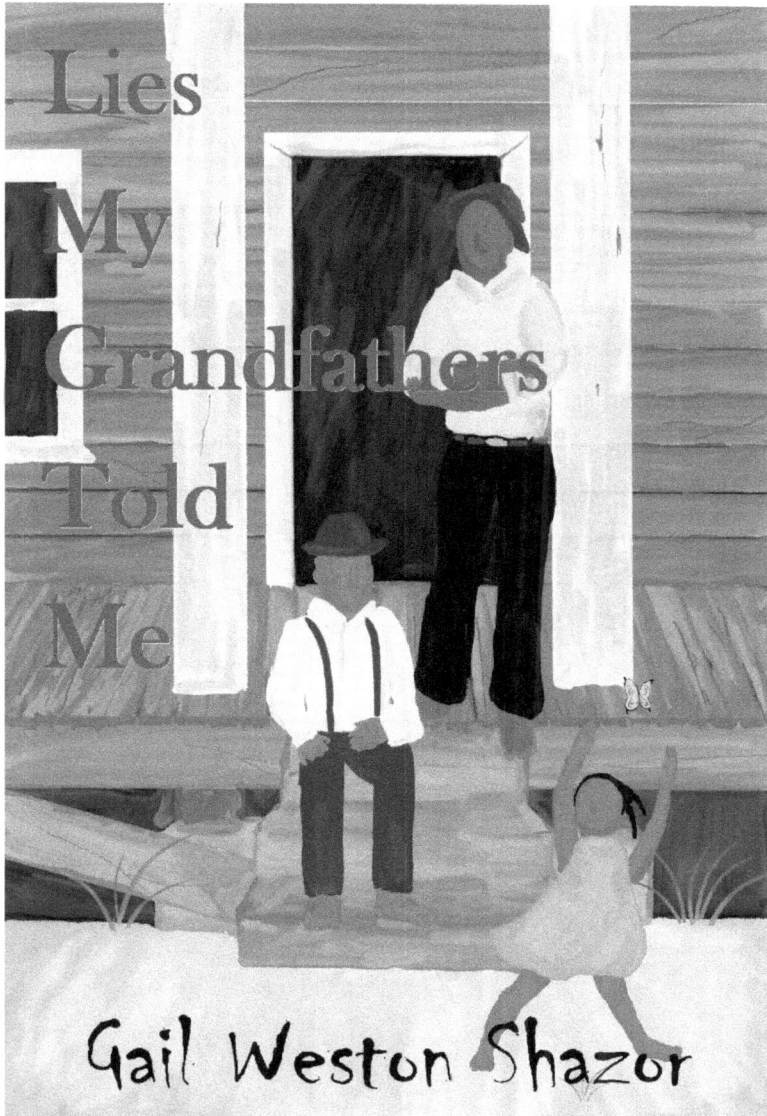

Lies
My
Grandfathers
Told
Me

Gail Weston Shazor

Aflame

Memoirs in Verse

hülya n. yılmaz

Now Available at
www.innerchildpress.com

Now Available at
www.innerchildpress.com

Breakfast

for

Butterflies

Faleeha Hassan

Now Available at
www.innerchildpress.com

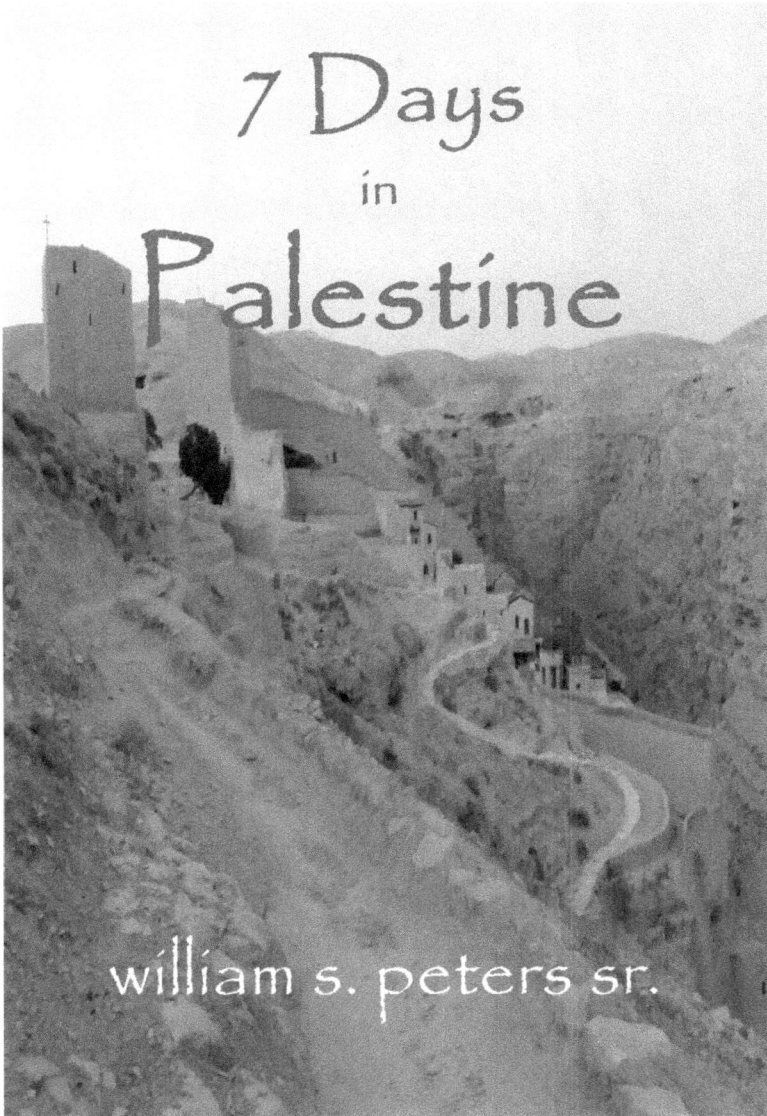

7 Days
in
Palestine

william s. peters sr.

Now Available at
www.innerchildpress.com

inner child press
presents

Tunisia My Love

william s. peters, sr.

Now Available at
www.innerchildpress.com

INNER CHILD PRESS

THIS IS WHY I
SLEEP

william s. peters sr.

Now Available at

www.innerchildpress.com

Think on These Things
Book II

william s. peters, sr.

Other

Anthological

works from

Inner Child Press International

www.innerchildpress.com

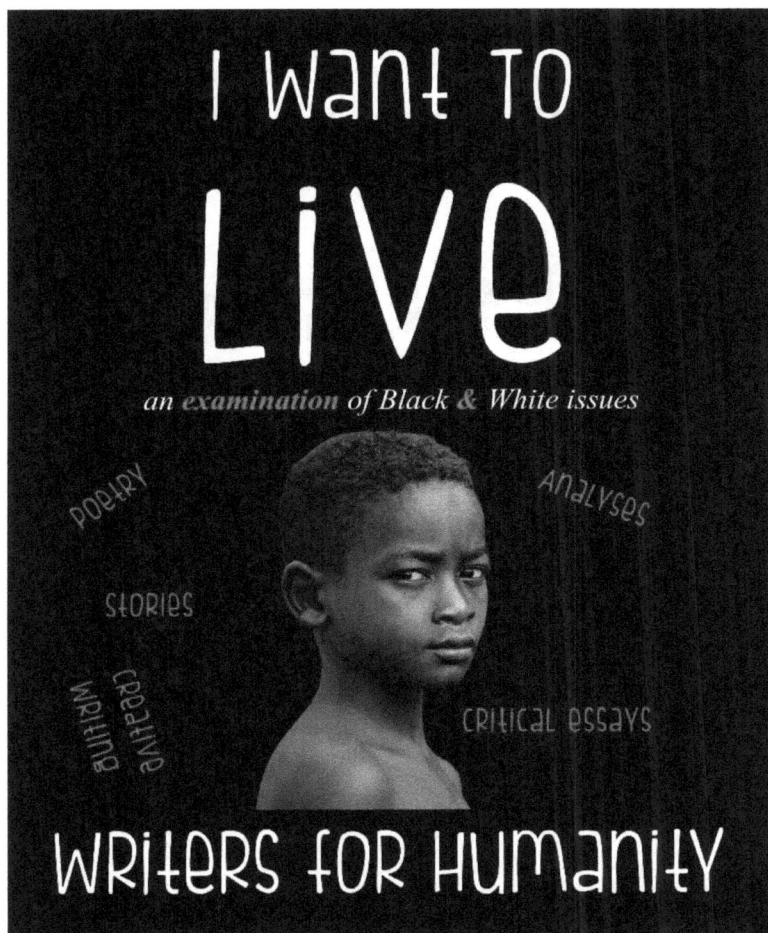

Now Available
www.innerchildpress.com

Inner Child Press International
&
The Year of the Poet
present

Poetry
the best of 2020

Poets of the World

Now Available
www.innerchildpress.com

Inner Child Press International

presents

W.A.R.

We Are Revolution

Poets for Humanity

Now Available
www.innerchildpress.com

the Heart of a Poet

words for a better tomorrow

The Conscious Poets

Now Available

www.innerchildpress.com

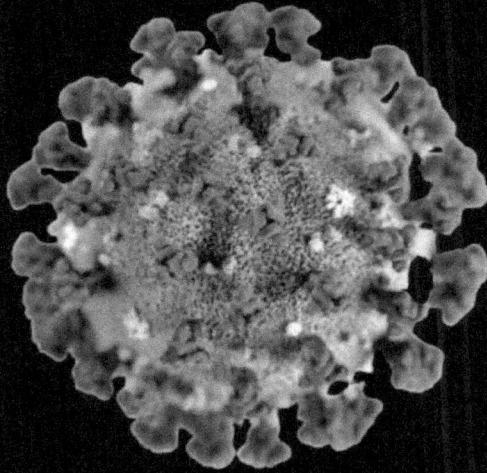

Corona

Social Distancing

Poets for Humanity

Now Available
www.innerchildpress.com

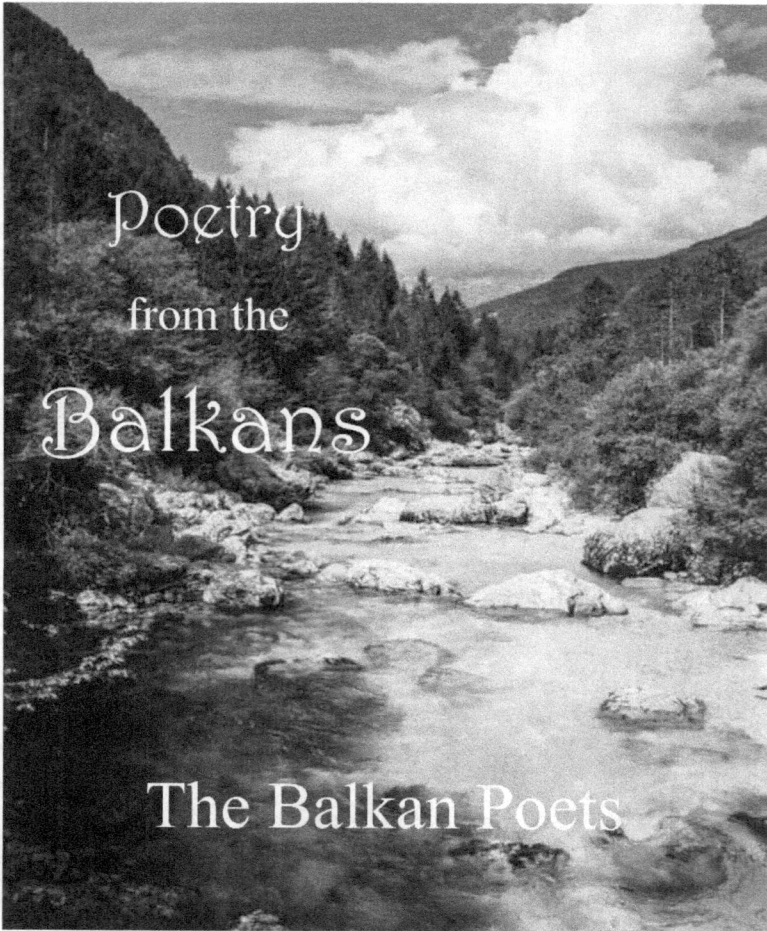

Poetry
from the
Balkans

The Balkan Poets

Now Available at
www.innerchildpress.com

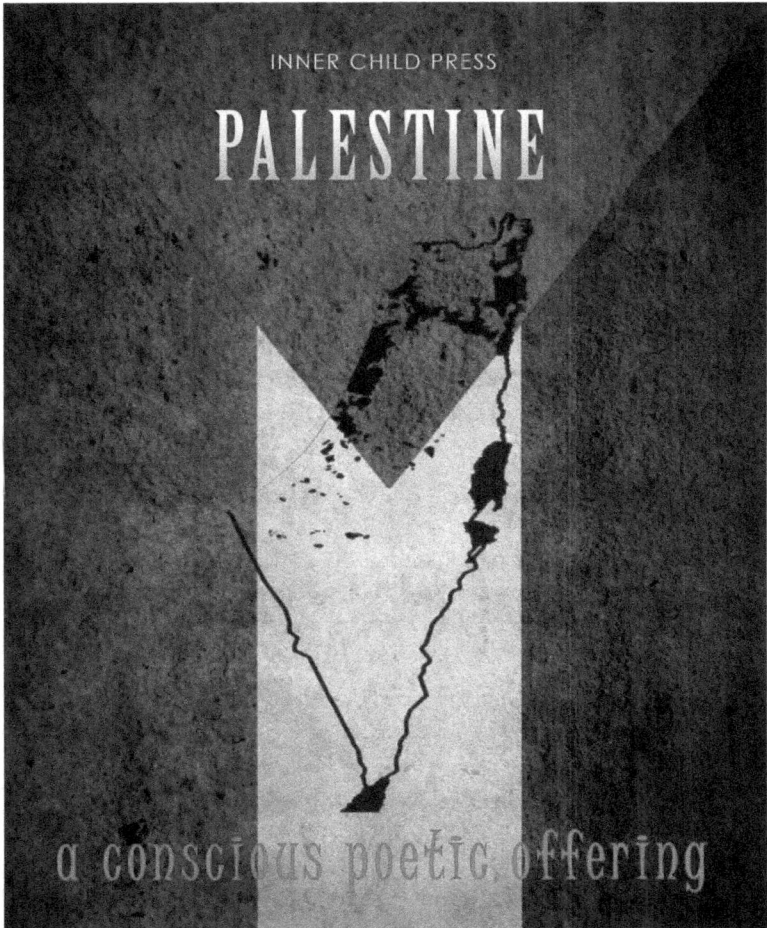

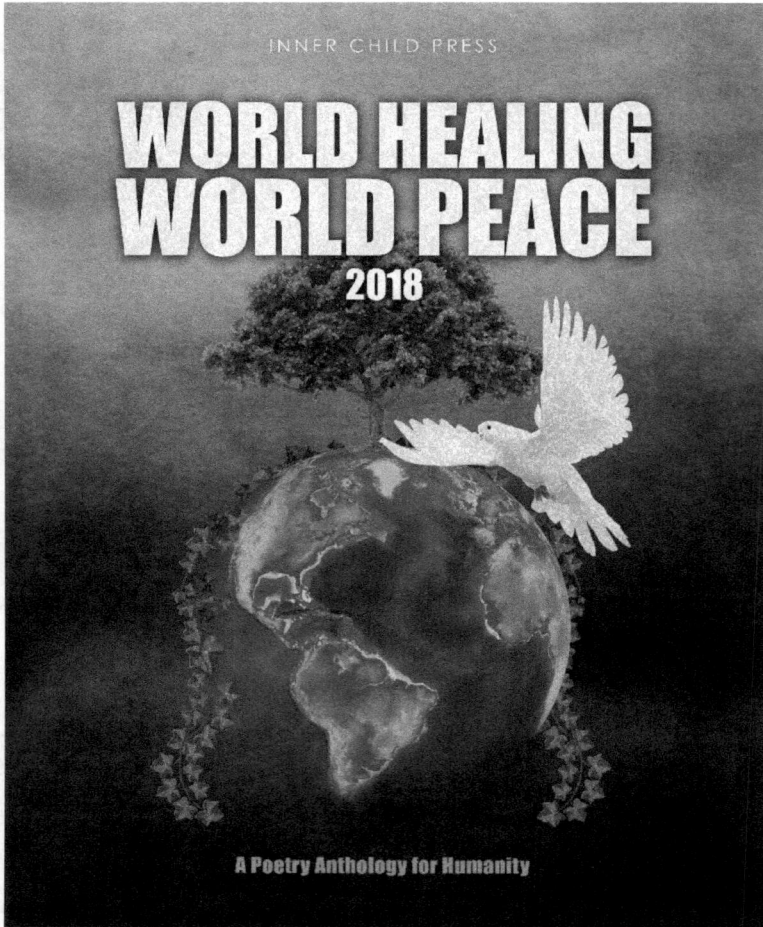

Now Available at

www.innerchildpress.com

Inner Child Press International
presents

A Love Anthology

2019

The Love Poets

Now Available

www.worldhealingworldpeacepoetry.com

185

Now Available

www.worldhealingworldpeacepoetry.com

World Healing World Peace
INNER CHILD PRESS
A Poetry Anthology 2014
Volume 1

World Healing World Peace
INNER CHILD PRESS
A Poetry Anthology 2014
Volume 2

World Healing World Peace
A POETRY ANTHOLOGY
Volume 1

World Healing World Peace
A POETRY ANTHOLOGY
Volume 2

Now Available

www.worldhealingworldpeacepoetry.com

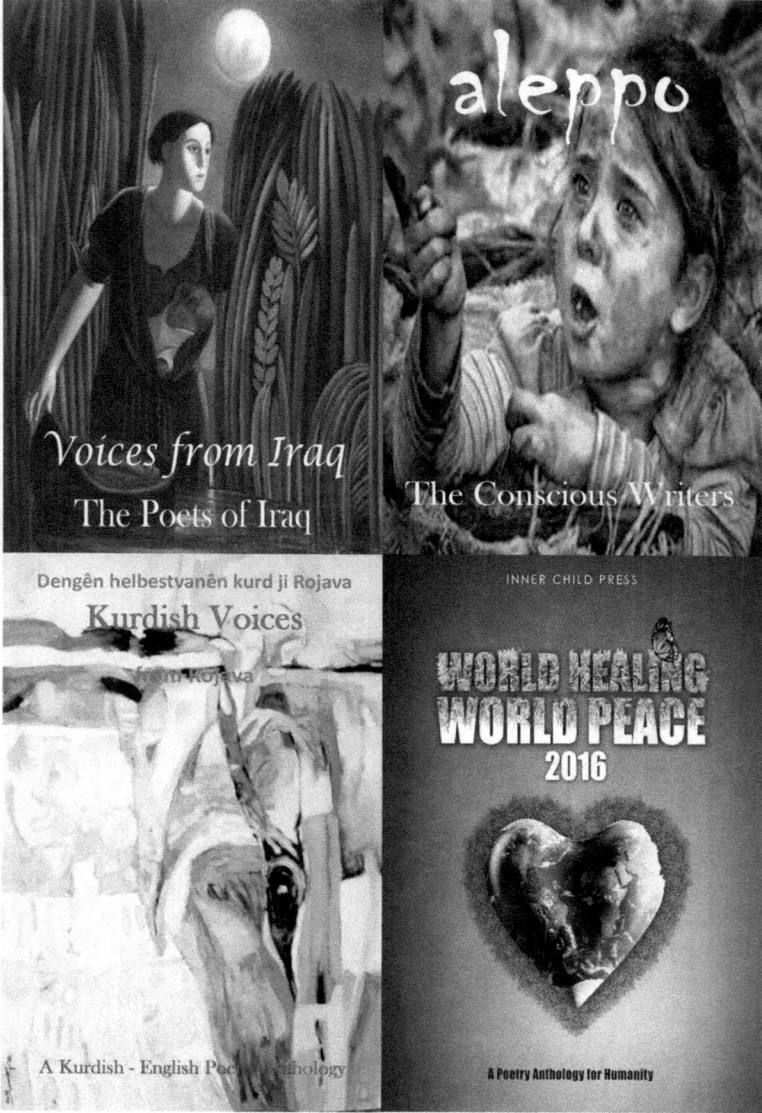

Now Available

www.innerchildpress.com/anthologies

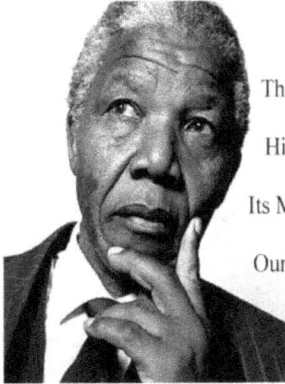

Mandela

The Man

His Life

Its Meaning

Our Words

Poetry . . . Commentary & Stories
The Anthological Writers

A GATHERING OF WORDS

POETRY & COMMENTARY
FOR
TRAYVON MARTIN

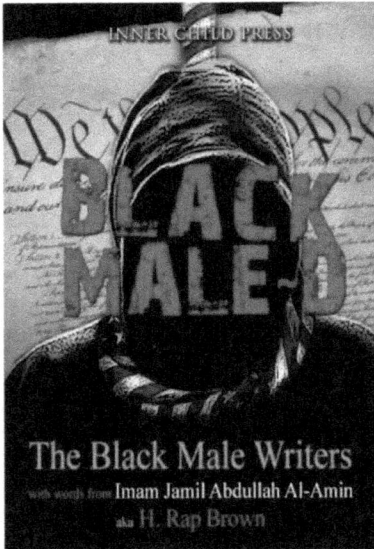

INNER CHILD PRESS

The Black Male Writers
with words from Imam Jamil Abdullah Al-Amin
aka H. Rap Brown

I
want
my
poetry
to... *volume* 4

the conscious poets
inspired by . . . Monte Smith

Now Available

Now Available

www.innerchildpress.com/anthologies

Now Available

www.innerchildpress.com/anthologies

a collection of the Voices of Many inspired by . . .

Monte Smith

volume II

volume 3

a collection of the Voices of Many inspired by . . .

Monte Smith

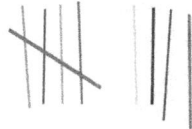

(9 lines . . .)

for those who are challenged

an anthology of Poetry inspired by . . .

Poetry Dancer

Now Available

www.innerchildpress.com/anthologies

The Year of the Poet
January 2014

The Poetry Posse

Jamie Bond
Gail Weston Shazor
Albert 'Infinite' Carrasco
Siddartha Beth Pierce
Janet P. Caldwell
June 'Bugg' Barefield
Debbie M. Allen
Tony Henninger
Joe DaVerbal Minddancer
Robert Gibbons
Neetu Wali
Shareef Abdur-Rasheed
William S. Peters, Sr.

Carnation

Our January Feature
Terri L. Johnson

the Year of the Poet
February 2014

violets

The Poetry Posse

Jamie Bond
Gail Weston Shazor
Albert 'Infinite' Carrasco
Siddartha Beth Pierce
Janet P. Caldwell
June 'Bugg' Barefield
Debbie M. Allen
Tony Henninger
Joe DaVerbal Minddancer
Robert Gibbons
Neetu Wali
Shareef Abdur-Rasheed
William S. Peters, Sr.

Our February Features
Teresa E. Gallion & Robert Gibson

the Year of the Poet
March 2014

The Poetry Posse

Jamie Bond
Gail Weston Shazor
Albert 'Infinite' Carrasco
Siddartha Beth Pierce
Janet P. Caldwell
June 'Bugg' Barefield
Debbie M. Allen
Tony Henninger
Joe DaVerbal Minddancer
Robert Gibbons
Neetu Wali
Shareef Abdur-Rasheed
Kimberly Burnham
William S. Peters, Sr.

daffodil

Our March Featured Poets
Alicia C. Cooper & hülya yılmaz

the Year of the Poet
April 2014

The Poetry Posse

Jamie Bond
Gail Weston Shazor
Albert 'Infinite' Carrasco
Siddartha Beth Pierce
Janet P. Caldwell
June 'Bugg' Barefield
Debbie M. Allen
Tony Henninger
Joe DaVerbal Minddancer
Robert Gibbons
Neetu Wali
Shareef Abdur-Rasheed
Kimberly Burnham
William S. Peters, Sr.

Our April Featured Poets
Fahredin Shehu
Martina Reisz Newberry
Justin Blackburn
Monte Smith

Sweet Pea

celebrating international poetry month

Now Available

www.innerchildpress.com/the-year-of-the-poet

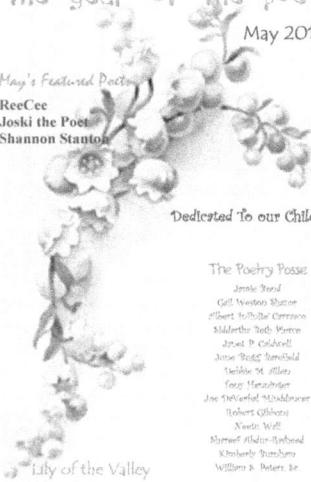

the year of the poet
May 2014

May's Featured Poets

ReeCee
Joski the Poet
Shannon Stanton

Dedicated to our Children

The Poetry Posse

Jamie Bond
Gail Weston Shazor
Albert Infinite Carrasco
Siddartha Beth Pierce
Janet P. Caldwell
Jamie Bugg Barefield
Debbie M. Allen
Tony Henninger
Joe DaVerbal Minddancer
Robert Gibbons
Neetu Wali
Shareef Abdur-Rasheed
Kimberly Burnham
William S. Peters, Sr.

Lily of the Valley

the Year of the Poet
June 2014

Love & Relationship

Rose

June's Featured Poets

Shantelle McLin
Jacqueline D. E. Kennedy
Abraham N. Benjamin

The Poetry Posse

Jamie Bond
Gail Weston Shazor
Albert Infinite Carrasco
Siddartha Beth Pierce
Janet P. Caldwell
Jamie Bugg Barefield
Debbie M. Allen
Tony Henninger
Joe DaVerbal Minddancer
Robert Gibbons
Neetu Wali
Shareef Abdur-Rasheed
Kimberly Burnham
William S. Peters, Sr.

The Year of the Poet
July 2014

July Feature Poets

Christena A. V. Williams
Dr. John R. Strum
Rolade Olanrewaju Freedom

The Poetry Posse

Jamie Bond
Gail Weston Shazor
Albert Infinite Carrasco
Siddartha Beth Pierce
Janet P. Caldwell
Jamie Bugg Barefield
Debbie M. Allen
Tony Henninger
Joe DaVerbal Minddancer
Robert Gibbons
Neetu Wali
Shareef Abdur-Rasheed
Kimberly Burnham
William S. Peters, Sr.

Lotus
Asian Flower of the Month

The Year of the Poet
August 2014

Gladiolus

The Poetry Posse

Jamie Bond
Gail Weston Shazor
Albert Infinite Carrasco
Siddartha Beth Pierce
Janet P. Caldwell
Jamie Bugg Barefield
Debbie M. Allen
Tony Henninger
Joe DaVerbal Minddancer
Robert Gibbons
Neetu Wali
Shareef Abdur-Rasheed
Kimberly Burnham
William S. Peters, Sr.

August Feature Poets

Ann White * Rosalind Cherry * Sheila Jenkins

Now Available

www.innerchildpress.com/the-year-of-the-poet

194

The Year of the Poet
September 2014

Aster   Morning-Glory

Wild Chestnut September Birth of Flower

September Feature Poets
Florence Malone * Keith Alan Hamilton

The Poetry Posse
Jamie Bond * Gail Weston Shazor * Albert Infinite Carrasco * Siddartha Beth Pierce
Janet P. Caldwell * June 'Bugg' Barefield * Debbie M. Allen * Tony Henninger
Joe DaVerbal Minddancer * Robert Gibbons * Neetu Wali * Shareef Abdur-Rasheed
Kimberly Burnham * William S. Peters, Sr.

THE YEAR OF THE POET
October 2014

Red Poppy

The Poetry Posse
Jamie Bond * Gail Weston Shazor * Albert Infinite Carrasco * Siddartha Beth Pierce
Janet P. Caldwell * June 'Bugg' Barefield * Debbie M. Allen * Tony Henninger
Joe DaVerbal Minddancer * Robert Gibbons * Neetu Wali * Shareef Abdur-Rasheed
Kimberly Burnham * William S. Peters, Sr.

October Feature Poets
Ceri Naz * RaJendra Padhi * Elizabeth Castillo

THE YEAR OF THE POET
November 2014

Chrysanthemum

The Poetry Posse
Jamie Bond * Gail Weston Shazor * Albert Infinite Carrasco * Siddartha Beth Pierce
Janet P. Caldwell * June 'Bugg' Barefield * Debbie M. Allen * Tony Henninger
Joe DaVerbal Minddancer * Robert Gibbons * Neetu Wali * Shareef Abdur-Rasheed
Kimberly Burnham * William S. Peters, Sr.

November Feature Poets
Jocelyn Mosman * Jackie Allen * James Moore * Neville Hiatt

THE YEAR OF THE POET
December 2014

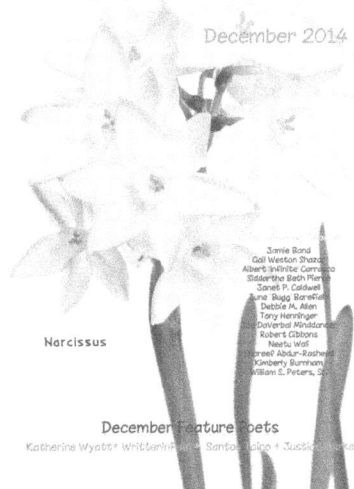

Narcissus

Jamie Bond
Gail Weston Shazor
Albert Infinite Carrasco
Siddartha Beth Pierce
Janet P. Caldwell
June 'Bugg' Barefield
Debbie M. Allen
Tony Henninger
Joe DaVerbal Minddancer
Robert Gibbons
Neetu Wali
Shareef Abdur-Rasheed
Kimberly Burnham
William S. Peters, Sr.

December Feature Poets
Katherine Wyatt * Writtenheart * Santosh Bhoomkar * Justice Pace

Now Available

www.innerchildpress.com/the-year-of-the-poet

The Year of the Poet II
January 2015

Garnet

The Poetry Posse
Jamie Bond
Gail Weston Shazor
Albert 'Infinite' Carrasco
Siddartha Beth Pierce
Janet P. Caldwell
Tony Henninger
Joe DaVerbal Minddancer
Robert Gibbons
Neetu Wali
Shareef Abdur – Rasheed
Kimberly Burnham
Ann White
Keith Alan Hamilton
Katherine Wyatt
Fahredin Shehu
Hülya N. Yılmaz
Teresa E. Gallion
Jackie Allen
William S. Peters, Sr.

January Feature Poets
Bismay Mohanti * Jen Walls * Eric Judah

THE YEAR OF THE POET II
February 2015

Amethyst

THE POETRY POSSE
Jamie Bond
Gail Weston Shazor
Albert 'Infinite' Carrasco
Siddartha Beth Pierce
Janet P. Caldwell
Tony Henninger
Joe DaVerbal Minddancer
Robert Gibbons
Neetu Wali
Shareef Abdur – Rasheed
Kimberly Burnham
Ann White
Keith Alan Hamilton
Katherine Wyatt
Fahredin Shehu
Hülya N. Yılmaz
Teresa E. Gallion
Jackie Allen
William S. Peters, Sr.

FEBRUARY FEATURE POETS
Iram Fatima * Bob McNeil * Kerstin Centervall

The Year of the Poet II
March 2015

Our Featured Poets
Heung Sook * Anthony Arnold * Alicia Poland

Bloodstone

The Poetry Posse 2015
Jamie Bond * Gail Weston Shazor * Albert 'Infinite' Carrasco
Siddartha Beth Pierce * Janet P. Caldwell * Tony Henninger
Joe DaVerbal Minddancer * Neetu Wali * Shareef Abdur – Rasheed
Kimberly Burnham * Ann White * Keith Alan Hamilton
Katherine Wyatt * Fahredin Shehu * Hülya N. Yılmaz
Teresa E. Gallion * Jackie Allen * William S. Peters, Sr

The Year of the Poet II
April 2015

Celebrating International Poetry Month
Our Featured Poets
Raja Williams · Dennis Ferado · Laure Charazac

Diamonds

The Poetry Posse 2015
Jamie Bond * Gail Weston Shazor * Albert 'Infinite' Carrasco
Siddartha Beth Pierce * Janet P. Caldwell * Tony Henninger
Joe DaVerbal Minddancer * Neetu Wali * Shareef Abdur – Rasheed
Kimberly Burnham * Ann White * Keith Alan Hamilton
Katherine Wyatt * Fahredin Shehu * Hülya N. Yılmaz
Teresa E. Gallion * Jackie Allen * William S. Peters, Sr.

Now Available

www.innerchildpress.com/the-year-of-the-poet

The Year of the Poet II
September 2015

Featured Poets

Alfreda Ghee · Lonneice Weeks Badley · Demetrios Trifiatis

Sapphires

The Poetry Posse 2015

Jamie Bond * Gail Weston Shazor * Albert 'Infinite' Carrasco
Siddartha Beth Pierce * Janet P. Caldwell * Tony Henninger
Joe DaVerbal Minddancer * Neetu Wali * Shareef Abdur – Rasheed
Kimberly Burnham * Ann White * Keith Alan Hamilton
Katherine Wyatt * Fahredin Shehu * Hülya N. Yılmaz
Teresa E. Gallion * Jackie Allen * William S. Peters, Sr.

The Year of the Poet II
October 2015

Featured Poets

Monte Smith * Laura J. Wolfe * William Washington

Opal

The Poetry Posse 2015

Jamie Bond * Gail Weston Shazor * Albert 'Infinite' Carrasco
Siddartha Beth Pierce * Janet P. Caldwell * Tony Henninger
Joe DaVerbal Minddancer * Neetu Wali * Shareef Abdur – Rasheed
Kimberly Burnham * Ann White * Keith Alan Hamilton
Katherine Wyatt * Fahredin Shehu * Hülya N. Yılmaz
Teresa E. Gallion * Jackie Allen * William S. Peters, Sr.

The Year of the Poet II
November 2015

Featured Poets

Alan W. Jankowski
Bismay Mohanty
James Moore

Topaz

The Poetry Posse 2015

Jamie Bond * Gail Weston Shazor * Albert 'Infinite' Carrasco
Siddartha Beth Pierce * Janet P. Caldwell * Tony Henninger
Joe DaVerbal Minddancer * Neetu Wali * Shareef Abdur – Rasheed
Kimberly Burnham * Ann White * Keith Alan Hamilton
Katherine Wyatt * Fahredin Shehu * Hülya N. Yılmaz
Teresa E. Gallion * Jackie Allen * William S. Peters, Sr.

The Year of the Poet II
December 2015

Featured Poets

Kerione Bryan * Michelle Joan Barulich * Neville Hiatt

Turquoise

The Poetry Posse 2015

Jamie Bond * Gail Weston Shazor * Albert 'Infinite' Carrasco
Siddartha Beth Pierce * Janet P. Caldwell * Tony Henninger
Joe DaVerbal Minddancer * Neetu Wali * Shareef Abdur – Rasheed
Kimberly Burnham * Ann White * Keith Alan Hamilton
Katherine Wyatt * Fahredin Shehu * Hülya N. Yılmaz
Teresa E. Gallion * Jackie Allen * William S. Peters, Sr.

Now Available

www.innerchildpress.com/the-year-of-the-poet

The Year of the Poet III
January 2016

Featured Poets

Lana Joseph * Atom Cyrus Rush * Christena Williams

Dark-eyed Junco

The Poetry Posse 2016

The Year of the Poet III
February 2016

Featured Poets

Anthony Arnold
Anna Chalasz
De Andre Hawthorne

Puffin

The Poetry Posse 2016

The Year of the Poet III
March 2016

Featured Poets

Jeton Kelmendi   Nizar Sartawi   Sami Muhanna

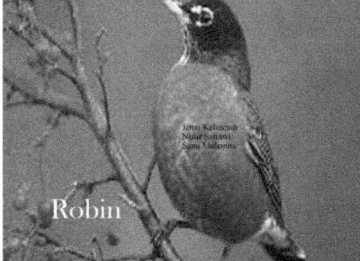

Robin

The Poetry Posse 2016

The Year of the Poet III

Featured Poets

Ali Abdolrezaei

Anna Chalasz

Agim Vinca

Ceri Naz

Black Capped Chickadee

The Poetry Posse 2016

celebrating international poetry month

Now Available

www.innerchildpress.com/the-year-of-the-poet

The Year of the Poet
May 2016

Bob Strum
Barbara Allan
D.L. Davis

Oriole

The Year of the Poet III
June 2016

Featured Poets

Qibrije Demiri- Frangu
Naime Beqiraj
Faleeha Hassan
Bedri Zyberaj

Black Necked Stilt

The Poetry Posse 2016

The Year of the Poet II
July 2016

Featured Poets

Tram Fatima 'Ashi'
Langley Shazor
Jody Doty
Emilia T. Davis

Indigo Bunting

The Poetry Posse 2016

The Year of the Poet III
August 2016

Featured Poets

Anita Dash
Irena Jovanovic
Malgorzata Gouluda

Painted Bunting

The Poetry Posse 2016

Now Available

www.innerchildpress.com/the-year-of-the-poet

The Year of the Poet III
September 2016

Featured Poets

Simone Weber
Abhijit Sen
Eunice Barbara C. Novio

Long Billed Curle

The Poetry Posse 2016

The Year of the Poet III
October 2016

Featured Poets

Lana Joseph
Uma Krishnamurthy R
James Moore

Barn Owl

The Poetry Posse 2016

The Year of the Poet III
November 2016

Featured Poets

Rosemary Burns
Robin Ouzman Hislop
Lonneice Weeks-Badley

Northern Cardinal

The Poetry Posse 2016

Gail Weston Shazor * Caroline Nazareno * Jen Walls
Nizar Sartawi * Janet P. Caldwell * Alfreda Ghee
Joe DaVerbal Minddancer * Shareef Abdur – Rasheed
Albert Carrasco * Kimberly Burnham * Elizabeth Castillo
Hülya N. Yılmaz * Demetrios Trifiatis * Albin W. Jankowski
Teresa E. Gallion * Jackie Davis Allen * William S. Peters, Sr.

The Year of the Poet III
December 2016

Featured Poets

Samih Masoud
Mountassir Aziz Bien
Abdulkadir Musa

Rough Legged Hawk

The Poetry Posse 2016

Gail Weston Shazor * Caroline Nazareno
Nizar Sartawi * Janet P. Caldwell * Alfreda Ghee
Joe DaVerbal Minddancer * Shareef Abdur – Rasheed
Albert Carrasco * Kimberly Burnham * Elizabeth Castillo
Hülya N. Yılmaz * Demetrios Trifiatis * Albin W. Jankowski
Teresa E. Gallion * Jackie Davis Allen * William S. Peters, Sr.

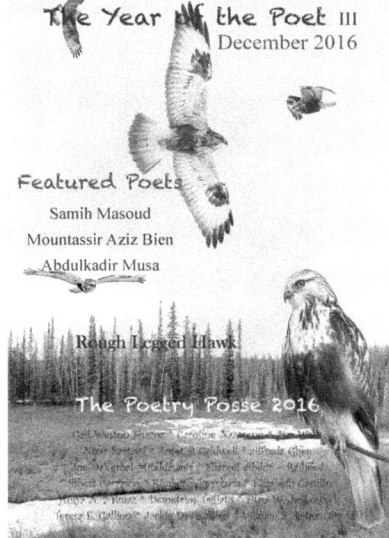

Now Available

www.innerchildpress.com/the-year-of-the-poet

The Year of the Poet IV
January 2017

Featured Poets

Jon Winell
Natalie Shields
Irani Fatima "Ashi"

Quaking Aspen

The Poetry Posse 2017

Gail Weston Shazor * Caroline Nazareno * Bismay Mohanty
Nizar Sartawi * Anna Jakubczak Vel Ratty Adalan * Jen Walls
Joe DeVerhal Misidancer * Shareef Abdur – Rasheed
Albert Carrasco * Kimberly Burnham * Elizabeth Castillo
Hülya N. Yılmaz * Faleeha Hassan * Alan W. Jankowski
Teresa E. Gallion * Jackie Davis Allen * William S. Peters, Sr.

The Year of the Poet IV
February 2017

Featured Poets
Lin Ross
Soukaina Fathi
Anwer Ghani

Witch Hazel

The Poetry Posse 2017

Gail Weston Shazor * Caroline Nazareno * Bismay Mohanty
Nizar Sartawi * Anna Jakubczak Vel Ratty Adalan * Jen Walls
Joe DeVerhal Misidancer * Shareef Abdur – Rasheed
Albert Carrasco * Kimberly Burnham * Elizabeth Castillo
Hülya N. Yılmaz * Faleeha Hassan * Alan W. Jankowski
Teresa E. Gallion * Jackie Davis Allen * William S. Peters, Sr.

The Year of the Poet IV
March 2017

Featured Poets
Tremell Stevens
Francisca Ricinski
Jamil Abu Shaih

The Eastern Redbud

The Poetry Posse 2017

Gail Weston Shazor * Caroline Nazareno * Bismay Mohanty
Teresa E. Gallion * Anna Jakubczak Vel Ratty Adalan
Joe DeVerhal Misidancer * Shareef Abdur – Rasheed
Albert Carrasco * Kimberly Burnham * Elizabeth Castillo
Hülya N. Yılmaz * Faleeha Hassan * Jackie Davis Allen
Jen Walls * Nizar Sartawi * * William S. Peters, Sr.

The Year of the Poet IV
April 2017

Featured Poets
Dr. Ruchida Barman
Neptune Barman
Masood Khalat

The Blossoming Cherry

The Poetry Posse 2017

Gail Weston Shazor * Caroline Nazareno * Bismay Mohanty
Teresa E. Gallion * Anna Jakubczak Vel Ratty Adalan
Joe DeVerhal Misidancer * Shareef Abdur – Rasheed
Albert Carrasco * Kimberly Burnham * Elizabeth Castillo
Hülya N. Yılmaz * Faleeha Hassan * Jackie Davis Allen
Jen Walls * Nizar Sartawi * * William S. Peters, Sr.

Now Available

www.innerchildpress.com/the-year-of-the-poet

The Year of the Poet IV
May 2017

The Flowering Dogwood Tree

Featured Poets
Kallisa Powell
Alicja Maria Kuberska
Fethi Sassi

The Poetry Posse 2017

The Year of the Poet IV
June 2017

Featured Poets
Eliza Segiet
Tze-Min Tsai
Abdulla Issa

The Linden Tree

The Poetry Posse 2017

The Year of the Poet IV
July 2017

Featured Poets
Anca Mihaela Bruma
Ibaa Ismail
Zvonko Taneski

The Oak Moon

The Poetry Posse 2017

The Year of the Poet IV
August 2017

Featured Poets
Jonathan Aquino
Kitty Hsu
Langley Shazor

The Hazelnut Tree

The Poetry Posse 2017

Now Available

www.innerchildpress.com/the-year-of-the-poet

The Year of the Poet IV
September 2017

Featured Poets

Martina Reisz Newberry
Ameer Nassir
Christine Fulco Neal
Robert Neal

The Elm Tree

The Poetry Posse 2017

Gail Weston Shazor * Caroline Nazareno * Bismay Mohanty
Teresa E. Gallion * Anna Jakubczak Vel Ratty Adalan
Joe DaVerbal Minddancer * Shareef Abdur – Rasheed
Albert Carrasco * Kimberly Burnham * Elizabeth Castillo
Hülya N. Yılmaz * Faleeha Hassan * Jackie Davis Allen
Jen Walls * Nizar Sartawi * * William S. Peters, Sr.

The Year of the Poet IV
October 2017

Featured Poets

Ahmed Abu Saleem
Nedal Al-Qaeim
Sadeddin Shahin

The Black Walnut Tree

The Poetry Posse 2017

Gail Weston Shazor * Caroline Nazareno * Bismay Mohanty
Teresa E. Gallion * Anna Jakubczak Vel Ratty Adalan
Joe DaVerbal Minddancer * Shareef Abdur – Rasheed
Albert Carrasco * Kimberly Burnham * Elizabeth Castillo
Hülya N. Yılmaz * Faleeha Hassan * Jackie Davis Allen
Jen Walls * Nizar Sartawi * * William S. Peters, Sr.

The Year of the Poet IV
November 2017

Featured Poets

Kay Peters
Alfreda D. Ghee
Gabriella Garofalo
Rosemary Cappello

The Tree of Life

The Poetry Posse 2017

Gail Weston Shazor * Caroline Nazareno * Bismay Mohanty
Teresa E. Gallion * Anna Jakubczak Vel Ratty Adalan
Joe DaVerbal Minddancer * Shareef Abdur – Rasheed
Albert Carrasco * Kimberly Burnham * Elizabeth Castillo
Hülya N. Yılmaz * Faleeha Hassan * Jackie Davis Allen
Jen Walls * Nizar Sartawi * William S. Peters, Sr.

The Year of the Poet IV
December 2017

Featured Poets

Justice Clarke
Mariel M. Pabroa
Kiley Brown

The Fig Tree

The Poetry Posse 2017

Gail Weston Shazor * Caroline Nazareno * Bismay Mohanty
Teresa E. Gallion * Anna Jakubczak Vel Ratty Adalan
Joe DaVerbal Minddancer * Shareef Abdur – Rasheed
Albert Carrasco * Kimberly Burnham * Elizabeth Castillo
Hülya N. Yılmaz * Faleeha Hassan * Jackie Davis Allen
Jen Walls * Nizar Sartawi * William S. Peters, Sr.

Now Available

www.innerchildpress.com/the-year-of-the-poet

The Year of the Poet V
January 2018

Featured Poets

Iyad Shamasnah

Yasmeen Hamzeh

Ali Abdolrezaei

Aksum

The Poetry Posse 2018

Gail Weston Shazor * Caroline Nazareno * Tezmin Ition Tsai
Hülya N. Yılmaz * Faleeha Hassan * Jackie Davis Allen
Teresa E. Gallion * Anna Jakubczak Vel Ratty Adalan
Alicja Maria Kuberska * Shareef Abdur – Rasheed
Kimberly Burnham * Elizabeth Castillo
Nizar Sartawi * William S. Peters, Sr.

The Year of the Poet V
February 2018

Sabean

Featured Poets

Muhammad Azram

Anna Szawrncka

Abhilipsa Kuanar

Aanika Aery

The Poetry Posse 2018

Gail Weston Shazor * Caroline Nazareno * Tezmin Ition Tsai
Hülya N. Yılmaz * Faleeha Hassan * Jackie Davis Allen
Teresa E. Gallion * Anna Jakubczak Vel Ratty Adalan
Alicja Maria Kuberska * Shareef Abdur – Rasheed
Kimberly Burnham * Elizabeth Castillo
Nizar Sartawi * William S. Peters, Sr.

The Year of the Poet V
March 2018

Featured Poets

Iram Fatima 'Ashi'
Cassandra Swan
Jaleel Khazaal
Shazia Zaman

Mexico   Cuba

Caribbean
&
Middle America

The Poetry Posse 2018

Gail Weston Shazor * Nizar Sartawi * Hülya N. Yılmaz
Jackie Davis Allen * Caroline 'Ceri' Nazareno
Alicja Maria Kuberska * Teresa E. Gallion
Faleeha Hassan * Shareef Abdur – Rasheed
Kimberly Burnham * Elizabeth Castillo
Tezmin Ition Tsai * William S. Peters, Sr.

The Year of the Poet V
April 2018

Featured Poets

The Nez Perce

The Poetry Posse 2018

Now Available

www.innerchildpress.com/the-year-of-the-poet

The Year of the Poet V
May 2018

Featured Poets

Zahily Carreon de Leon Jr.
Sylwia K. Malinowska
Lindita Ahmeti
Ofelia Product

The Sumerians

The Poetry Posse 2018

Gail Weston Shazor * Nizar Sartawi * Hülya N. Yılmaz
Jackie Davis Allen * Caroline 'Ceri' Nazareno
Alicja Maria Kuberska * Teresa E. Gallion
Kimberly Burnham * Shareef Abdur – Rasheed
Faleeha Hassan * Elizabeth Castillo * Swapna Behera
Tezmin Ition Tsai * William S. Peters, Sr.

The Year of the Poet V
June 2018

Featured Poets

Bilall Maliqi * Daim Miftari * Gojko Božović * Sofija Živković

The Paleo Indians

The Poetry Posse 2018

Gail Weston Shazor * Nizar Sartawi * Hülya N. Yılmaz
Jackie Davis Allen * Caroline 'Ceri' Nazareno
Alicja Maria Kuberska * Teresa E. Gallion
Kimberly Burnham * Shareef Abdur – Rasheed
Faleeha Hassan * Elizabeth Castillo * Swapna Behera
Tezmin Ition Tsai * William S. Peters, Sr.

The Year of the Poet V
July 2018

Featured Poets

Padmaja Iyengar-Paddy
Mohammad Ikbal Harb
Eliza Segiet
Tom Higgins

Oceania

The Poetry Posse 2018

Gail Weston Shazor * Nizar Sartawi * Hülya N. Yılmaz
Jackie Davis Allen * Caroline 'Ceri' Nazareno
Alicja Maria Kuberska * Teresa E. Gallion
Kimberly Burnham * Shareef Abdur – Rasheed
Faleeha Hassan * Elizabeth Castillo * Swapna Behera
Tezmin Ition Tsai * William S. Peters, Sr.

The Year of the Poet V
August 2018

Featured Poets
Hussein Habasch * Mircea Dan Duta * Naida Mujkić * Swagat Das

The Lapita

The Poetry Posse 2018

Gail Weston Shazor * Nizar Sartawi * Hülya N. Yılmaz
Jackie Davis Allen * Caroline 'Ceri' Nazareno
Alicja Maria Kuberska * Teresa E. Gallion
Kimberly Burnham * Shareef Abdur – Rasheed
Ashok K. Bhargava* Elizabeth Castillo * Swapna Behera
Tezmin Ition Tsai * William S. Peters, Sr.

Now Available

www.innerchildpress.com/the-year-of-the-poet

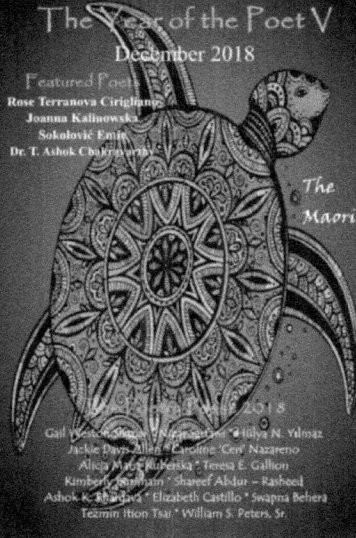

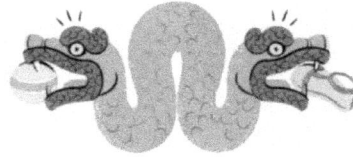

The Year of the Poet VI
September 2019
Featured Poets
Elena Liliana Popescu * Gobinda Biswas
Iram Fatima 'Ashi' * Joseph S. Spence, Sr.

The Caucasus
The Poetry Posse 2019
Gail Weston Shazor * Albert Carrasco * Hülya N. Yılmaz
Jackie Davis Allen * Caroline Nazareno * Eliza Segiet
Alicja Maria Kuberska * Teresa E. Gallion * Joe Paire
Kimberly Burnham * Shareef Abdur – Rasheed
Ashok K. Bhargava * Elizabeth Castillo * Swapna Behera
Tezmin Ition Tsai * William S. Peters, Sr.

The Year of the Poet VI
October 2019
Featured Poets
Ngozi Olivia Osuoha * Denisa Kondié
Pankhuri Sinha * Christena AV Williams

The Nile Valley
The Poetry Posse 2019
Gail Weston Shazor * Albert Carrasco * Hülya N. Yılmaz
Jackie Davis Allen * Caroline Nazareno * Eliza Segiet
Alicja Maria Kuberska * Teresa E. Gallion * Joe Paire
Kimberly Burnham * Shareef Abdur – Rasheed
Ashok K. Bhargava * Elizabeth Castillo * Swapna Behera
Tezmin Ition Tsai * William S. Peters, Sr.

The Year of the Poet VI
November 2019
Featured Poets
Rozalie Aleksandrova * Orbindu Ganga
Smruti Ranjan Mohanty * Sofia Skleida

Northern Asia
The Poetry Posse 2019
Gail Weston Shazor * Albert Carrasco * Hülya N. Yılmaz
Jackie Davis Allen * Caroline Nazareno * Eliza Segiet
Alicja Maria Kuberska * Teresa E. Gallion * Joe Paire
Kimberly Burnham * Shareef Abdur – Rasheed
Ashok K. Bhargava * Elizabeth Castillo * Swapna Behera
Tezmin Ition Tsai * William S. Peters, Sr.

The Year of the Poet VI
December 2019
Featured Poets
Rakim Karim * Sujoy Paik
Bharati Nayak * Kapardeli Eftichia

Oceania
The Poetry Posse 2019
Gail Weston Shazor * Albert Carrasco * Hülya N. Yılmaz
Jackie Davis Allen * Caroline Nazareno * Eliza Segiet
Alicja Maria Kuberska * Teresa E. Gallion * Joe Paire
Kimberly Burnham * Shareef Abdur – Rasheed
Ashok K. Bhargava * Elizabeth Castillo * Swapna Behera
Tezmin Ition Tsai * William S. Peters, Sr.

Now Available

www.innerchildpress.com/the-year-of-the-poet

210

The Year of the Poet VII
January 2020

Featured Poets
B S Tyagi * Ashok Chakravarthy Tholana
Andy Scott * Anwer Ghani

1901 Jean Henry Dunant and Frédéric Passy

The Year of Peace
Celebrating past Nobel Peace Prize Recipients

The Poetry Posse 2020
Gail Weston Shazor * Albert Carasco * Hülya N. Yılmaz
Jackie Davis Allen * Caroline Nazareno * Eliza Segiet
Alicja Maria Kuberska * Teresa E. Gallion * Joe Paire
Kimberly Burnham * Shareef Abdur – Rasheed
Ashok K. Bhargava * Elizabeth Castillo * Swapna Behera
Tezmin Ition Tsai * William S. Peters, Sr.

The Year of the Poet VII
February 2020

Featured Poets
Jennifer Ades * Martina Reisz Newberry
Ibrahim Honjo * Claudia Piccinno

Henri La Fontaine ~ 1913

The Year of Peace
Celebrating past Nobel Peace Prize Recipients

The Poetry Posse 2020
Gail Weston Shazor * Albert Carasco * Hülya N. Yılmaz
Jackie Davis Allen * Caroline Nazareno * Eliza Segiet
Alicja Maria Kuberska * Teresa E. Gallion * Joe Paire
Kimberly Burnham * Shareef Abdur – Rasheed
Ashok K. Bhargava * Elizabeth Castillo * Swapna Behera
Tezmin Ition Tsai * William S. Peters, Sr.

The Year of the Poet VII
March 2020

Featured Poets
Aziz Mountassir * Krishna-Paraisa
Hannie Rouweler * Rozalia Aleksandrova

Aristide Briand ~ 1926 ~ Gustav Stresemann

The Year of Peace
Celebrating past Nobel Peace Prize Recipients

The Poetry Posse 2020
Gail Weston Shazor * Albert Carasco * Hülya N. Yılmaz
Jackie Davis Allen * Caroline Nazareno * Eliza Segiet
Alicja Maria Kuberska * Teresa E. Gallion * Joe Paire
Kimberly Burnham * Shareef Abdur – Rasheed
Ashok K. Bhargava * Elizabeth Castillo * Swapna Behera
Tezmin Ition Tsai * William S. Peters, Sr.

The Year of the Poet VII
April 2020

Featured Poets
Rohini Behera * Mircea Dan Duta
Monalisa Dash Dwibedy * NilavroNill Shoovro

Carlos Saavedra Lamas ~ 1936

The Year of Peace
Celebrating past Nobel Peace Prize Recipients

The Poetry Posse 2020
Gail Weston Shazor * Albert Carasco * Hülya N. Yılmaz
Jackie Davis Allen * Caroline Nazareno * Eliza Segiet
Alicja Maria Kuberska * Teresa E. Gallion * Joe Paire
Kimberly Burnham * Shareef Abdur – Rasheed
Ashok K. Bhargava * Elizabeth Castillo * Swapna Behera
Tezmin Ition Tsai * William S. Peters, Sr.

Now Available

www.innerchildpress.com/the-year-of-the-poet

211

The Year of the Poet VII
May 2020
Featured Poets
Alok Kumar Ray * Eden S. Trinidad
Franco Barbato * Izabela Zubko

Ralph Bunche ~ 1950

The Year of Peace
Celebrating past Nobel Peace Prize Recipients

The Poetry Posse 2020
Gail Weston Shazor * Albert Carasco * Hülya N. Yılmaz
Jackie Davis Allen * Caroline Nazareno * Eliza Segiet
Alicja Maria Kuberska * Teresa E. Gallion * Joe Paire
Kimberly Burnham * Shareef Abdur – Rasheed
Ashok K. Bhargava * Elizabeth Castillo * Swapna Behera
Tezmin Ition Tsai * William S. Peters, Sr.

The Year of the Poet VII
June 2020
Featured Poets
Eftichia Kapardeli * Metin Cengiz
Hussein Habasch * Kosh K Mathew

Albert John Lutuli ~ 1960

The Year of Peace
Celebrating past Nobel Peace Prize Recipients

The Poetry Posse 2020
Gail Weston Shazor * Albert Carasco * Hülya N. Yılmaz
Jackie Davis Allen * Caroline Nazareno * Eliza Segiet
Alicja Maria Kuberska * Teresa E. Gallion * Joe Paire
Kimberly Burnham * Shareef Abdur – Rasheed
Ashok K. Bhargava * Elizabeth Castillo * Swapna Behera
Tezmin Ition Tsai * William S. Peters, Sr.

The Year of the Poet VII
July 2020
Featured Poets
Mykola Martyniuk * Orbindu Ganga
Roula Pollard * Karn Praktisha

Norman Ernest Borlaug ~ 1970

The Year of Peace
Celebrating past Nobel Peace Prize Recipients

The Poetry Posse 2020
Gail Weston Shazor * Albert Carasco * Hülya N. Yılmaz
Jackie Davis Allen * Caroline Nazareno * Eliza Segiet
Alicja Maria Kuberska * Teresa E. Gallion * Joe Paire
Kimberly Burnham * Shareef Abdur – Rasheed
Ashok K. Bhargava * Elizabeth Castillo * Swapna Behera
Tezmin Ition Tsai * William S. Peters, Sr.

The Year of the Poet VII
August 2020
Featured Poets
Dr Pragya Suman * Chinh Nguyen
Srinivas Vasudev * Ugwu Leonard Ifeanyi, Jr.

Adolfo Pérez Esquivel ~ 1980

The Year of Peace
Celebrating past Nobel Peace Prize Recipients

The Poetry Posse 2020
Gail Weston Shazor * Albert Carasco * Hülya N. Yılmaz
Jackie Davis Allen * Caroline Nazareno * Eliza Segiet
Alicja Maria Kuberska * Teresa E. Gallion * Joe Paire
Kimberly Burnham * Shareef Abdur – Rasheed
Ashok K. Bhargava * Elizabeth Castillo * Swapna Behera
Tezmin Ition Tsai * William S. Peters, Sr.

Now Available

www.innerchildpress.com/the-year-of-the-poet

The Year of the Poet VII

September 2020

Featured Poets

Raed Anis Al-Jishi * Soibinarni Soiejano
Dr. Bragosh Kumar Gupta * Unsil Najjari

Mikhail Sergeyevich Gorbachev ~ 1990

The Year of Peace
Celebrating past Nobel Peace Prize Recipients

The Poetry Posse 2020

Gail Weston Shazor * Albert Carasco * Hülya N. Yılmaz
Jackie Davis Allen * Caroline Nazareno * Eliza Segiet
Alicja Maria Kuberska * Teresa E. Gallion * Joe Paire
Kimberly Burnham * Shareef Abdur – Rasheed
Ashok K. Bhargava * Elizabeth Castillo * Swapna Behera
Tezmin Ition Tsai * William S. Peters, Sr.

The Year of the Poet VII

October 2020

Featured Poets

Mutawaf A. Shaheed * Galina Italyanskaya
Nadeem Fraz * Avril Tanya Meallem

Kim Dae-jung ~ 2000

The Year of Peace
Celebrating past Nobel Peace Prize Recipients

The Poetry Posse 2020

Gail Weston Shazor * Albert Carasco * Hülya N. Yılmaz
Jackie Davis Allen * Caroline Nazareno * Eliza Segiet
Alicja Maria Kuberska * Teresa E. Gallion * Joe Paire
Kimberly Burnham * Shareef Abdur – Rasheed
Ashok K. Bhargava * Elizabeth Castillo * Swapna Behera
Tezmin Ition Tsai * William S. Peters, Sr.

The Year of the Poet VII

November 2020

Featured Poets

Elisa Mascia * Sue Lindenberg McClelland
Hani Janabi * Ivan Gacina

Liu Xiaobo ~ 2010

The Year of Peace
Celebrating past Nobel Peace Prize Recipients

The Poetry Posse 2020

Gail Weston Shazor * Albert Carasco * Hülya N. Yılmaz
Jackie Davis Allen * Caroline Nazareno * Eliza Segiet
Alicja Maria Kuberska * Teresa E. Gallion * Joe Paire
Kimberly Burnham * Shareef Abdur – Rasheed
Ashok K. Bhargava * Elizabeth Castillo * Swapna Behera
Tezmin Ition Tsai * William S. Peters, Sr.

The Year of the Poet VII

December 2020

Featured Poets

Ratan Ghosh * Ibtisam Ibrahim Al-Asady
Brindha Vinodh * Selma Kopic

Abiy Ahmed Ali ~ 2019

The Year of Peace
Celebrating past Nobel Peace Prize Recipients

The Poetry Posse 2020

Gail Weston Shazor * Albert Carasco * Hülya N. Yılmaz
Jackie Davis Allen * Caroline Nazareno * Eliza Segiet
Alicja Maria Kuberska * Teresa E. Gallion * Joe Paire
Kimberly Burnham * Shareef Abdur – Rasheed
Ashok K. Bhargava * Elizabeth Castillo * Swapna Behera
Tezmin Ition Tsai * William S. Peters, Sr.

Now Available

www.innerchildpress.com/the-year-of-the-poet

213

and there is much, much more !

visit . . .

www.innerchildpress.com/antho
logies-sales-special.php

Also check out our Authors and all the wonderful Books Available at :

www.innerchildpress.com/autho
rs-pages

World Healing World Peace
2020

Poets for Humanity

Now Available

www.worldhealingworldpeacepoetry.com

INNER CHILD PRESS

WORLD HEALING WORLD PEACE
2018

A Poetry Anthology for Humanity

Now Available

www.worldhealingworldpeacepoetry.com

support

World Healing
World Peace

www.worldhealingworldpeacepoetry.com

World Healing **World Peace**

World Healing
World Peace
2012, 2014, 2016, 2018, 2020

Now Available

www.worldhealingworldpeacepoetry.com

Inner Child Press International

'building bridges of cultural understanding'

Meet the Board of Directors

www.innerchildpress.com

Inner Child Press International

'building bridges of cultural understanding'

Meet our Cultural Ambassadors

Fahredin Shehu
Director of Cultural

Faleha Hassan
Iraq – USA

Elizabeth E. Castillo
Philippines

Antoinette Coleman
Chicago
Midwest USA

Ananda Nepali
Nepal - Tibet
Northern India

Kimberly Burnham
Pacific Northwest
USA

Alicja Kuberska
Poland
Eastern Europe

Swapna Behera
India
Southeast Asia

Kolade O. Freedom
Nigeria
West Africa

Monsif Beroual
Morocco
Northern Africa

Ashok K. Bhargava
Canada

Teemin Ition Tsai
Republic of China
Greater China

Alicia M. Ramírez
Mexico
Central America

Christena AV Williams
Jamaica
Caribbean

Louise Hudon
Eastern Canada

Aziz Mountassir
Morocco
Northern Africa

Shareef Abdur-Rasheed
Southeastern USA

Laure Charazac
France
Western Europe

Mohammad Ikbal Harb
Lebanon
Middle East

**Mohamed Abdel
Aziz Shmeis**
Egypt
Middle East

Hilary Mainga
Kenya
Eastern Africa

Josephus R. Johnson
Liberia

www.innerchildpress.com

This Anthological Publication
is underwritten solely by

Inner Child Press International

Inner Child Press is a Publishing
Company Founded and Operated by
Writers. Our personal publishing
experiences provides us an intimate
understanding of the sometimes daunting
challenges Writers, New and Seasoned
may face in the Business of Publishing
and Marketing their Creative "Written
Work".

For more Information

Inner Child Press International

www.innerchildpress.com

'building bridges of cultural understanding'
202 Wiltree Court, State College, Pennsylvania 16801

www.innerchildpress.com

~ fini ~

www.ingramcontent.com/pod-product-compliance
Lightning Source LLC
LaVergne TN
LVHW051045080426
835508LV00019B/1716